ershop

PART I

By Jeff Grissler & Eric Ryant

D1382473

2013 Edition

Books by Jeff Grissler and Eric Ryant
Ready Set Go Publishing, LLC

Ready, Set, Go! The Start-Up Guide for Opening, Remodeling, & Running a Successful Barbershop
© 2012 Jeff Grissler and Eric Ryant. All Rights Reserved.

Find other Ready Set Go series books on www.salonresourceguide.com

First edition.

Published in the U.S. by Ready Set Go Publishing, LLC
215 Pascal Street
Fort Collins Colorado 80524

Printed in the United States of America

ISBN 978-0-9855802-7-8

About the Authors

Jeff Grissler has been where you are and understands the inner workings of the hair industry and what leads to success as a salon or barbershop owner. As a business owner himself, he knows the business landscape and what owners can expect and guides them to success. Jeff is a partner of and the National Sales Manager for Quest Resources—one of the hair industry's leading financing companies for furniture and equipment. His career in finance actually began on Wall Street and he has been involved in the multimillion dollar hair and beauty industry for over 20 years. Jeff has financed over 15,000 salons and barbershops to help them open their doors

or complete their remodeling project through creative financing strategies. Published in many hair and beauty trade magazines, Jeff is setting a new business standard in the hair industry as we see it today. Jeff has a portfolio of over 600 million dollars in salon and barbershop financing and a network of over 150 manufacturers, distributors, and vendors. A gifted businessman and consultant, Jeff prides himself on his networking ability to bring people together to share new ideas and explore partnerships and marketing techniques. Through his skilled negotiations, he has convinced the banking industry to lift restrictions from the hair and beauty industry. He has also negotiated contracts and leases with salon/barbershop owners, spa owners, distributors, manufacturers, and banking management.

Jeff was born in New York City before moving to the Jersey Shore. He was a New York City fireman for 15+ years and served during 911. Jeff now resides in Wilmington, NC with his wife, Coleen, and their three children—Kaytlyn, JT, and Julianna Rose. Jeff offers consulting services to current salon/barbershop owners and to those who have ownership of a salon, barbering, nail, or spa business in their near-term or future career plans. To reach Jeff, you can contact him directly at jgrissler@questrs.com.

Eric Ryant is a beauty industry entrepreneur with over 30 years of experience in space planning and design for salons and barbershops. No stranger to the hair and beauty industry, Eric spent many years developing new designs and space plans, getting involved in every facet of the industry. Since the 1980s, Eric has imported salon and barbering furniture from many countries, such as Italy, Germany, Holland, and China, bringing in the latest trends and styles for the U.S. market. Prior to writing this book, Eric owned several successful businesses, all involved in the hair and beauty industry, from a small chain of beauty stores to a cabinet manufacturing facility. He has also collaborated with companies such as Sally Beauty Supply, L'Oreal and The Nailco Group.

Eric's vision is to help business owners to create their dreams with a cost-effective business model and ensure that they stay within budget for the long haul. As part of his successful career, he now teaches and consults with other organizations on how to achieve the same success. Eric can be reached at ericryant@gmail.com.

Acknowledgements

Jeff Grissler

You never really understand how important your friends and family are until you take on a large project. My wife, Coleen, was my sounding board and always had insightful feedback. I can't tell you how much I appreciated her support and encouragement. My children, Kaytlyn, JT, and Julianna are always an inspiration and fill my life with joy. I also can never forget to mention mom and dad for always believing in me and never doubting my dreams and sometimes crazy ideas.

To Jason Frye at Teakettle Junction Productions for his writing and editing help. To Robin Krauss at Linden Design for his expert help putting the book together.

Eric Ryant

First and foremost, I want to thank my mother, Cynthia. She has always been the backbone of the family and even though I don't express it as much as I should, I do love her dearly. To my father, Harvey, who passed many years ago, thanks for watching over me. To my children, Chase, Kendall, and Sloane, just know that anything is possible and writing this second book is proof again that anything is possible when you put your mind to it.

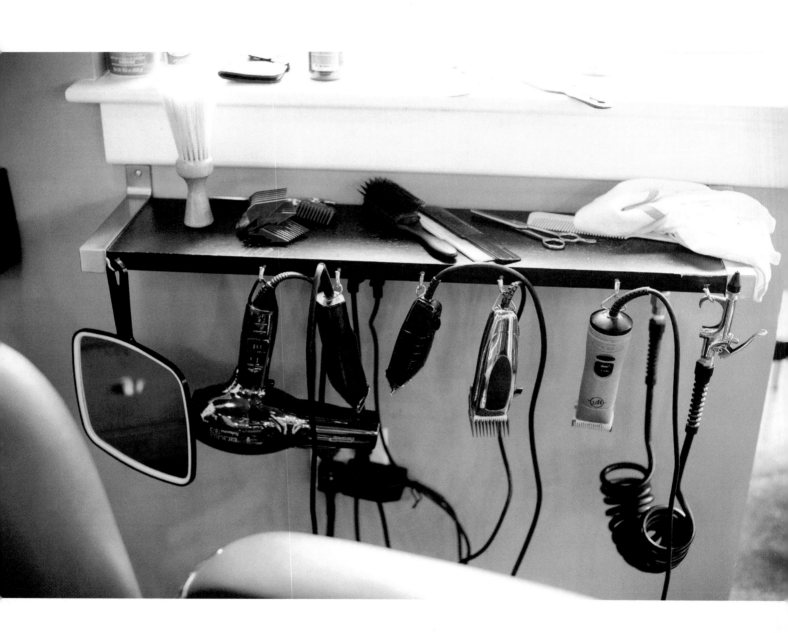

"Memories are made in the barbershop. I'm happy to see that the old days of father and son visiting the barber to get coiffed is back in style. The time for well-groomed gentleman is here. Barbershops and men's grooming lounges are reclaiming the male client and treating him like a king. This is where the well-groomed man has gone for decades, but now it's back—bigger and better than ever. Not only do men get some much needed man time, they also get the added confidence of knowing that they'll look their best.

I travel coast-to-coast all year long sharing fundamentals with beauty professionals. The barbering boom is on the rise—I see it all over, both in the heart of the city and in the suburbs. Men are spending more time and getting more services than ever before on themselves to get the look they want. This is the greatest time ever to become the place where men want to go and indulge in grooming services.

That's right! Men want to look great and take care of their hair, nails, and skin—and, they are willing to pay for it. Men have a new awareness about taking care of themselves. The men's 'spa' is no longer a luxury, it is a necessity.

This book is certainly timely, giving new barbershop owners the ideas, plans, and strategies for opening a successful barbering business. Jeff and Eric have done it again and provided another outstanding resource to the industry. Veteran barbershop owners can also look to this book for remaking their current barbering business into one that better fits the trends and client expectations."

Geno Stampora - Consultant & Speaker

INTRODUCTION

The Barber Industry Today As We See It

Barbershops are back. Through good and bad economic times, barbershops have always been a part of the multi-billion dollar haircare and beauty industry, but in the last few years, they've made a comeback. What makes barbershops and salons more resistant to uncertain economic times than other industries? And why are barbershops continuing to increase in popularity and profitability? The answer is easy – vanity.

In today's world, men and women want to appear younger and more attractive, feel good about how they look and find a place to pamper them. For many men and women, salons and spas offer what they want, but a growing number of men are looking for barbershops to provide these services.

Think about it. The barbers of yesteryear offered more than a buzz cut, they pampered men – regular trims; hot shaves; neck, scalp and facial massages; even manicures and color treatments. Today, the best barbershops offer these services to their clients and they're thriving.

We want you to thrive too, that's why we've written this book. In *Ready, Set, Go! Barbershop Success – The How-To Guide for Opening & Remodeling a Barbershop*, you'll find all the information you need to open a new or remodel an existing barbershop. We cover selecting a location,real estate leases, setting up your business, selecting and purchasing equipment, leasing and financing, and walk you through some of what to expect for your first year in business.

The book you're holding in your hands right now is the most comprehensive business-building guide in the men's grooming industry. We've filled the book with advice, checklists, and quotes from barbershop owners and operators around the world, putting the tools and advice you need to succeed at your fingertips.

TABLE OF CONTENTS

INTRODUCTION

Table of Contents

Part III: Financing

Part IV: Appendices

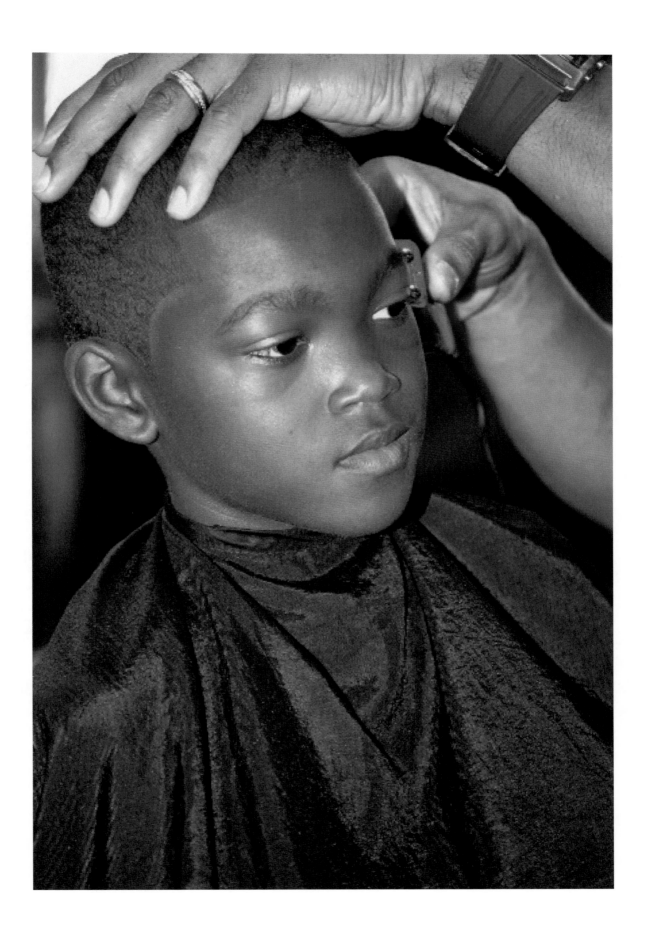

CHAPTER 1

How & Why to Become a Barber

"If you are going to be a champion, you must be willing to pay a greater price."

—Bud Wilkinson

For the male barber reading this book, I am sure you remember your first "official" haircut. Maybe it was like a scene from a Norman Rockwell painting. First, the barber put a booster seat in the chair. Then, he gently placed his young client in the seat, covered you with a huge apron, and started what seemed to be the longest haircut in the world. One of your parents likely grabbed the first fallen locks of hair and placed them in a plastic bag to cherish forever. There may have been a few tears shed; both by you and probably your mother. Wow, what a memory.

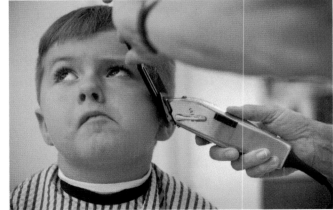

In fact, this memory probably influenced you to start a career in barbering. Thinking back on it now do you think that the barber from your early days as a young boy seemed happy? Was his barbershop clean? Was the barbershop located right in the heart of town? Did it seem to be the local gathering spot for all to meet and socialize while the barber continued to work?

Do you remember the barber himself being greeted like the mayor or a social leader in the community? I remember my first barber and it seemed like he knew about everything going on in town. If you wanted to know what high school won the football game, who just got a big promotion, or what new player your favorite sports team picked up, you asked your barber.

For the female barber reading this book, did your dad, grandpa, or uncle take you along to get his haircut at his favorite barbershop? As you are remembering back to those days, can you still smell the tonic powder and aftershave? What about the sounds of the clippers buzzing? Do you remember the before and after image of your dad, grandpa, or uncle? Do you remember how much he enjoyed his time at the barber?

We have witnessed a growing trend in females applying for barber school and entering the workplace over the past decade. It is not uncommon to see as many female barbers as men in barbershops around the world today. Women can dominate in an industry that has been predominantly run by men.

Statistics Don't Lie

What has motivated you to work in the barbering industry?

It seems like the world is searching for the right job with the right security in this very tough economic climate. According to the Bureau of Labor Statistics (BLS), "Employment of hairdressers, hairstylists, and cosmetologists is projected to grow 16 percent, about as fast as the average for all occupations. Demand for hair coloring, hair straightening, and other advanced hair treatments has increased in recent years, a trend that is expected to continue over the coming decade." The number of new barbers entering the work force will be less than 10 percent. Opportunities for barbers are still good.

Most job openings will result from those who transferred to another occupation, retired, or left the labor force for other reasons. However, workers or future barbershop owners can expect keen competition for jobs. Finding good, reliable barbers will be harder as the economy gets better and the existing barbershops try to hire the best barbers in the area. In 2010, the BLS reported 62,200 licensed barbers in the United States. The BLS expects a seven percent change in barbers with the number growing to 66,700 licensed barbers by 2020.

Your earning potential will be considerably higher than most professionals entering the job market, and will naturally grow as you become more experienced or open your own barbershop. The key to your success will be the ability to attract and hold regular clients.

The popularity of the local barber is once again becoming the building block of the community. Landlords and real estate companies welcome the fact that you may want to open a barbershop in their town or strip mall. They realize the need for this type of service. It is a fact that hair salons and barbershops are becoming serious anchors in real estate projects around the country.

Education & Training

All states require barbers and other personal appearance workers to be licensed. To qualify for a valid state barber license, most job seekers must graduate from a licensed barber or cosmetology school. Some states require that you have a diploma from high school or a GED before you can in enroll in their barbering programs. You must be at least 16 years of age to enroll. Programs in hairstyling and barbering can be found in public or private vocational schools.

The schooling and duration of a barber program can vary greatly, depending on your state's requirements. There are some programs that last 10 months, while others can take up to 16 months to complete the full requirements.

The amount of class hours varies widely. You must have actual class time, sometimes as much as 400 hours, before you actually cut hair. You will be working on mannequins before you work on a real person's hair. Most schools have an active area where the public can come in and get discounted hair services from the students who are attending the school. This gives students the opportunity to work on human clients as their skills progress over the course of their schooling. These experiences are ideal because it gives students the time needed to meet their requirements and cut hair under the supervision and guidance of a state-licensed teacher who is trained in cosmetology or barbering.

Besides focusing on the practical hair styling or barbering techniques used today, listed below are the requirements that you will be expected to understand before you can graduate:

- State laws and requirements
- Personal hygiene
- Professional ethics
- Business operation
- Fashion, art, and technical design
- People skills (very important for those wishing to open their own barbershops)
- Grooming products and how they are used
- Anatomy
- Razor cutting
- Bacteriology, sanitation
- Hair cutting and hair treatments
- Shaving
- Sales and marketing

Barbering Schools Costs

Barbering school costs differ from state to state. In most cases, the courses are offered on a full- and part-time basis. So, that can change the overall price. As you begin to look at schools that interest you, ask how much they cost and what requirements are needed to enroll. If you need a student loan, they should be able to guide you through that process with the school administrator.

Vocational schools and private barbering colleges vary significantly depending on school, state, and area. The website www.costhelper.com lists ranges from $2,500 to $15,000 for barbering schools around the country.

Grants for Barber Schools

The idea of becoming a barber is a great step for your future, but you may not have the financial capacity to obtain your dream. This is where grants come in. Many grant programs exist and are available to assist students with obtaining the monies needed to enroll in barbering school.

Pell Grants are one type of financial aid provided directly by the federal government to help with education. Pell Grants are need-based grants to help cover tuition and fees; and, most times, grant recipients do not need to pay them back. For the past five years, grants have been ranging from four to six thousand dollars.

These grants can be used to cover the costs of going to an approved trade school for barbering. There are about 5,500 participating schools around the country. You must fill out the application and get approved for the grant. Most states have barbering schools that are approved and eligible to receive Pell Grants.

Obtaining Your License

Once you have graduated from your barbering course, you will be expected to take a state licensing examination. The exam consists of a written test and/or an oral examination. A fee is usually required upon application for a license to become a barber. Once you pass your test and pay your licensing fee, you are ready to start your barbering career.

Why did you choose barbering as your career?

○ For job security

○ To be a leader in the community

○ To eventually own my own barbershop

○ To build a business to hand down to my kids

○ To encourage my staff and educate men about the importance of good grooming

○ To continue the barbering tradition

THE GOOD, THE BAD & THE UGLY

(Brought to you by barbershop and salon owners and other industry leaders)

American Haircuts, Wallace Barlow, Director of Education, Global Educator/Platform Artist for Woody's Quality Grooming, Educator/Platform Artist for The Andis Company

"I had worked/trained in upscale Aveda salon and spas producing 2-2.5 million dollars a year. I sort of went through a period of wanting to redefine my career. So, I got back into the men's barbering industry when I relocated to Atlanta, GA. I came across American Haircuts/Metro Men's Grooming through a contact I had and have been with American Haircuts for several years now."

The Ultimate Barber Lounge, Tone McGill, Charlotte, NC

"My father had a pair of clippers laying around the house that he used on both of us. When he wasn't around, I tried cutting my own hair and to my surprise the haircut turned out pretty good. I then started cutting family and friends for free. Shortly after getting started, I began charging. I turned the basement of my house into a barbershop at the age of 13 and would cut hair after school and on the weekends. This provided a good income for a kid with no bills and living at home with his parents. For me, barbering became a way to make money and buy new clothes."

Clean and Mean Men's Cutz, Atlanta, GA

"I was undecided on what I wanted to do with my life. I always liked my barber. I had gotten my haircuts from him my whole life. He gave everyone advice, including me. He knew everyone in town and they loved him. When he passed, I decided I would be that guy.

I went to barbering school and now own my barbershop. I have eight great barbers who work for me. I am working daily on becoming the man that I looked up to my whole life, a leader in the community. My shop has now become a place where kids hang out, talk sports, life, and becoming men. I encourage school and education. I am trying daily to become my old friend: my favorite barber!"

Ivan Zoot, Andis Company, Director of Education and Customer Engagement

Q: Why is barbering a good career?

A: "Ongoing demand throughout your lifetime. This service cannot be computerized! Cannot cut hair on the web! Good, solid income. Positive lifestyle. Positive social interaction daily. Lots of reasons."

Star Barbers, Dallas Texas

"No matter how bad the economy, everyone needs a haircut. I chose barbering because of the need factor. I needed money and men and women needed haircut!"

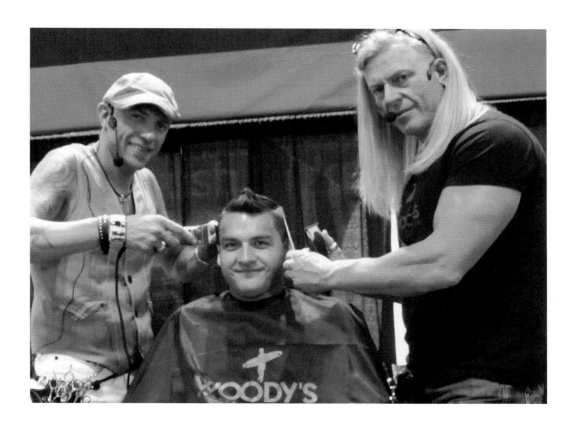

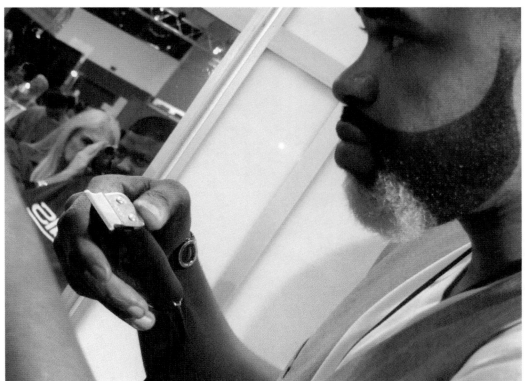

CHAPTER 2

Getting Started

"He who is not courageous enough to take risks will accomplish nothing in life."

—Muhammad Ali

The opportunity in men's grooming and barbering is yours for the taking! It's up to you to decide if owning your own men's grooming or barbershop is right for you at this point in your career. If you are contemplating the ownership of your own barbershop, then your head is probably swimming with questions, such as:

- Where do I begin?
- What is the first step?
- Who do I talk to?
- Where do I find the staff?
- Is the risk worth the reward?
- Do I want all the responsibilities?
- Do I have enough capital?
- Do I have the management skills?
- Do I have the ability?

As you can see, there are so many questions and so many different aspects to consider. You will not only be cutting hair, but managing people, purchasing product, marketing your business—the list of new duties and responsibilities goes on and on. But, we are here to tell you—it is possible and all it takes is planning and guidance.

Ready, Set, Go! is a guide to assist you in creating a successful men's grooming or barbering business. This book is meant to prepare you mentally for what you can expect as a business owner, how to get a handle on the financial obligations, and help you properly plan and navigate the process of opening or renovating your business so that you have a greater chance for success. We are going to take you through a step-by-step process to give you concepts and guidance that will sustain a long-term, profitable operation. After all, the purpose for owning and operating your barbering business is to make money, right?

What is the outlook for barbering and men's grooming? It is booming! Why?

Why this sudden return to the modernized barbershop? A lot of factors come into play, but consider this:

1. **Employability**—Given the turbulent state of the job market, men want to appear younger. Men are concerned about their livelihood and they are searching for a youth serum. Your barbershop can offer the services needed to keep the man of today looking young and fresh for their career. Companies want and need experience; they also want to know that their "aging" employees are in touch with the times. It shows flexibility, adaptability, and a willingness to change. Being fifty is nifty, but looking thirty is even better. Creating a youthful, hip look can be critical for the aging man to find new pursuits in his workplace. Keeping an aura of youth can add years to a man's career, keeping them gainfully employed and living the lifestyle to which they are accustomed.

2. **Culture of Vanity**—Men fall under the same pressures and enforcement of standards as woman when it comes to looks, aging, and style. Everybody wants to look their best, but most everyone has flaws that they want to work on or fix. The anti-aging craze is getting bigger and bigger. According to the Los Angeles Times, 1.5 million plastic surgeries were performed on men last year in the United States alone, which included face lifts, nose reshaping, eyelid surgery, and liposuction—not to mention hair transplants. Outside of the hospital, men are heading to men's grooming shops and barbershops on a more frequent basis looking to upgrade their look in new and remarkable ways.

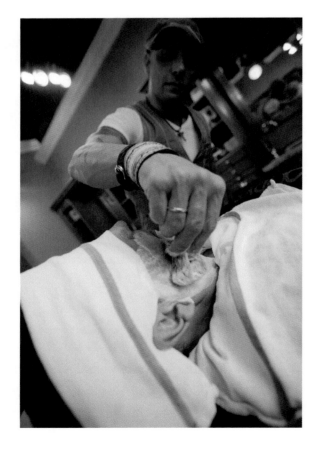

3. **Fighting the Aging Process**—Father Time wears on everyone all and when it

catches up to you, it can leave you looking old and tired. Nobody can stop the process completely, but the barbering industry can help put the brakes on aging and keep the men of today looking and feeling good. Putting a cap on the aging process is impossible, but you have the opportunity to capture one of the fastest growing men's grooming trends in the world today.

4. **Millennium Man**—Men have grown up accustomed to woman telling them what to do with their appearance. But, it's not about a haircut and looking clean shaven anymore. It's about a whole new look for the millennium man of today. Gone is the worry that mom always wanted us to be clean shaven and look neat with a fresh haircut.

5. **Seeking the Ultimate Grooming Experience**—Men are looking for a place with a 1920s country-club vibe that combines the community and nostalgia of an old barbershop, outstanding customer service, and professionalism. These grooming locations should have a masculine feel where a man can relax, unwind, and confidently enjoy the highest quality haircut, shave, or spa service in town. The services men are asking for are no longer limited to a haircut, buzz cut, or facial shave. This booming business has opened the door for more services and product sales. The barber of yesteryear did not even think about offering the types of services and products that men want from today's grooming experience.

Can You Beat the Odds?

Undoubtedly, the question of whether you can beat the odds is probably the biggest question on your mind. It's good that you ask yourself this question. You must not fool yourself and we don't want you to walk into this without the full picture of what it takes to open or renovate a barbershop. It's a fact that the industry has one of the highest rates of business failure. Opening a barbershop and investing in a renovation or relocation project, takes planning, capital, and business management skills. For some barbershops, the profit is so small that the owners make the same amount of money that they did when they worked for someone else. Only now, they have the additional responsibilities and pressure of being a business owner.

Almost all business failures (no matter what industry) can be attributed to poor management, insufficient capital, or lack of experience. In most cases, the business owner:

- Opened in an area crowded with competing businesses
- Did not offer services that their target market wanted or needed
- Did not change when local market conditions changed
- Did not have sufficient capital to sustain the business
- Lacked knowledge in these matters:
  1. Accounting
  2. Profit margins

3. Employee relations
4. Finances
5. Marketing
6. Purchasing and retailing

A lack of knowledge results in the inability to come up with the right answers when faced with operating decisions. That is why some entrepreneurs leaving barbering school look for a franchise, such as: Sport Clips, Supercuts, Kennedy's Barber Club, and American Male as a way to open up their first barbershop business. Many franchises offer training programs, ongoing management assistance, and a proven track record of success. While franchises are not guaranteed, the percentage of success is much greater than independent startups that learn by trial and error.

So, before deciding to open a barbershop, you have to make a commitment to doing what it will take to be successful. That may mean that you'll have to put off your plans to begin until you've saved more money or found a way to raise more capital. It might also mean that you need to return to school and take some general business classes through your local college or university.

Deciding Factors

Let's look at the deciding factors that will help you determine whether you are ready to open your own salon business.

Start by looking at the pros and cons of owning and operating your own salon.

	PRO	CON
1	You get to make all the decisions.	When the decision is wrong, you have to live with the consequences.
2	You get to create the client or guest experience that you want.	You must lead others with your vision to help them provide this experience.
3	You can design and furnish the barbershop to your liking.	You have to pay for it out of your own financial capital and stick to your budget.
4	You can open a barbershop close to where you live.	If there are too many barbershops (or salons) in the area where you live, you will have to look elsewhere.
5	You'll have employees working for you.	Your employees are relying on you to run a successful business and help with their growth and development.
6	Your income has endless possibilities.	You must pay your employees before you pay yourself.
7	The hours of operation are your choice.	You will be working long hours and time off is limited.

Next, consider your experience. Have you worked long enough in a barbershop or in the hair industry? Working for someone else gives you an overall sense of what goes on in the business each day and what you can expect. When you graduate from barbering school, you normally will not have the clients or the business experience to own and operate your own barbershop. Skills and creativity do not ensure that you will be a successful business owner. The benefit of working in a barbershop (or a salon that serves male clients) allows you the time to grow as a person, build your clientele, and learn from your mistakes while working and getting paid by someone else. We recommend that you get a job in a barbershop that is in the geographical area in which you want to eventually open your business.

Having the proper education and experience in barbering and men's grooming is vital to your success, but business owners also need to use computers proficiently. And, they also need a basic understanding of marketing, accounting, and finance. We suggest that you take a few computer and business courses at a local community college to learn the skills needed to run your business. Understanding the bottom line and how a business works is critical to success.

Are You Ready?

The next step is to ask yourself some questions about your current situation, your job, and your financial position.

Look at your current job and ask yourself:

- ○ Does your job give you a good retirement plan, health insurance, and vacation?
- ○ Do you like the security of working for someone and is that more important to you than owning your own barbershop?
- ○ Do you like your job?
- ○ Do you like your boss and coworkers?
- ○ Would you be happier just switching jobs or actually starting your own business?
- ○ Are you afraid of risk?
- ○ Do you think you can make more money if you open your own business?
- ○ Do you have basic computer skills?
- ○ Have you had experience managing people?
- ○ Do you have the business management skills to run a business?
- ○ Can you envision what success looks like and get other people on board to help you fulfill your vision?
- ○ Do you manage yourself well during times of stress or uncertainty?

Remember, when you open your business, everything becomes your responsibility and your decisions and your actions will affect not only you, but your staff as well.

If you find that you are indeed satisfied with your current job or that you still need more experience, then this book will assist you on your career potential as a barbershop owner in the future. Solidify your foundation first, build your clientele, and begin educating yourself for the future.

However, if you have found that you have what it takes to start your own barbering business, then read on. You will find that this book is the most comprehensive start-up and learning guide for getting ready to embark on building a successful barbershop and achieving your career goals and earning potential.

Entrepreneurial Self-Test

To help you decide if opening your own barbershop is truly the right move for you, take this test. Answer honestly and figure out your score based on the information given below to assist you in uncovering more information about yourself and your abilities to own and operate a successful barbershop.

Please rate these questions 1 to 5 (1 being lowest and 5 highest)

		1	2	3	4	5
1.	I seek opportunities all the time.	1	2	3	4	5
2.	look toward the future, not the past.	1	2	3	4	5
3.	I am committed to being the best.	1	2	3	4	5
4.	I am market-driven and customer-oriented.	1	2	3	4	5
5.	I value employees and I am willing to develop them.	1	2	3	4	5
6.	I am tolerant of small tasks.	1	2	3	4	5
7.	I don't accept failure.	1	2	3	4	5
8.	I am realistic.	1	2	3	4	5
9.	I am decisive and focused.	1	2	3	4	5
10.	I have business management experience.	1	2	3	4	5

Scoring Breakdown

1. If you score less than 25 points, we recommend that you get a job in a progressive, growing salon in your area which will set the stage to take this test again in a year.

2. If your score is between 25 and 35 points, we recommend that you concentrate on your work ethic and take some more courses on self-development or business.

3. If your score is more than 35 points, you may be ready to take the next step. There is no guarantee, but the opportunity to succeed with drive and determination is a possibility.

It is important to realize that this test is just one way of knowing whether you have the motivation and drive to start your own business. You need to realize that the current world is a quick-paced, ever-changing market and what worked well yesterday may not work well today. As a business owner, you must be a good listener and learner, always open to new ideas and concepts. Success comes from doing everything well rather than just doing a few things exceptionally well.

As Tom Smith, president of Food Lion grocery stores stated, "We don't try to be 1,000 percent better on a few things; we try to be one percent better on 1,000 things."

You have to be better. And to be better, you must have the courage, ability, and the commitment to your business and your customers.

CHAPTER 3

The American Dream

"Going into business for yourself, becoming an entrepreneur, is the modern-day equivalent of pioneering on the old frontier."
—Paula Nelson

The *American Dream* is about building a better life for yourself and having the opportunity to succeed based on your aspirations and your abilities. Most people fulfill this dream through their careers or business ownership.

Millions of Americans will choose to go to work for a company that will provide regular paychecks, a sense of security, health insurance, retirement savings plans, etc. While many will be content working for someone else, others want something more. They want to be in charge of their own destiny. They aspire to own and run their own business.

Over 600,000 new businesses opened all over the country last year. Excited entrepreneurs of all ages did exactly what they needed to do to start their business. They planned, plotted, borrowed, and invested so that they could open and build their own successful business. Many are winning, doing well, making a profit, and living the life of an entrepreneur.

Here is a story of one business owner and how her barbershop, Nathanael's, came into existence:

> *Diana Arellanes began her career in the hair industry 21 years ago. She worked for a chain salon for 7½ years, and then was inspired to move to a private salon. She was there for 3½ years, when a vision came to her to open her own barbershop, and the idea of Nathanael's came to be a dream, with God providing open doors and lots of blessings. Nathanael's opened its doors March 27, 2001 to serve clients and make them feel good about themselves. A dream came true.*

What makes people like Diana different? Do they have a crystal ball that allows them to predict the future or is it that they see things differently than most people?

New entrepreneurs simply look at the economy and figure out a way to take the best advantage of the opportunity that exists. The new entrepreneurs are finding solutions and reshaping the way people did business in the past so that it's successful in the present and positioned for the future. They are showing people in the world that they can open a business, buy a building, hire people, and operate a business.

Is this you? Do you want something more out of your job and career? Have you decided that owning a business and being an entrepreneur is your destiny? If your answer is, "YES!" then, "Congratulations!" But, before you read on in this book, take a minute to really describe what you want and what you envision for your barbershop. This will be helpful when you are presented with different options for your barbershop. You can always go back to what you envision and work toward creating that vision from this point forward.

Remember, in life, it is up to you to create your own destiny and fulfill your goals. But, you can't just have goals; you must plan and do something to achieve them!

This is My IDEAL Barbershop . . .

When I break down what I envision, my barbershop will . . .

Look like . . .	
Sound like . . .	
Feel like . . .	

I want to open a barbershop because:

○ I want to provide the best barbering and grooming services for men in the area.

○ I want my shop to be the sports information center for my town, where all the guys come for their sports fix and a good haircut.

○ Creating is my life.

○ Hair care is my life.

○ I would like to educate and develop the best barbering team in the country.

○ I think a barber is vital to a community.

○ My barbershop will be a welcoming place in the community.

○ Men need a place where they feel like they can relax and be themselves.

○ People will come to my place of business because they feel welcome.

○ I want my shop to be a place where my male clients can escape from the everyday trials and tribulations of life.

○ I want to be part of carrying on the tradition of barbering.

○ I want my clients to look good and feel good about their hair.

When clients come to my barbershop for the first time, they will:

Say . . .	
Feel . . .	
Think . . .	

Employees of my barbershop will:

Say . . .	
Feel . . .	
Think . . .	

PART II

PLANNING

CHAPTER 4

Why Men's Grooming Is Booming

In today's world—with the most turbulent job market in the history of our country—men are trying to figure out how to look younger. According to the Los Angeles Times, 1.5 million plastic surgeries were performed on men last year, the majority of which were facelifts. Nose reshaping, eyelid surgery, liposuction, and hair transplants constituted a large part of the other surgeries performed on men.

Outside of the hospital, men are heading to men's grooming salons and barbershops on a more frequent basis and upgrading their look in new and remarkable ways. No longer are they worrying about their mom's approval and always wanting them to be clean-shaven with freshly trimmed hair. Men, from the time they were boys, were accustomed to women telling them what to do with their appearance. But, it's not just about a haircut and being clean-shaven anymore. It's about a whole new look and creating the man of the millennia.

This man is searching for a youth serum. Your barbershop or grooming salon can offer the services needed to keep today's man looking young and fresh for their pursuits. Creating this youthful, hip look can be critical for the aging man looking for a new career or workplace. Companies want and need experience, but they also want to know that they are hiring individuals who are in touch with the times and even the fashions and trends of today. Being fifty is nifty, but looking thirty is even better. Keeping an aura of youth can add years to a man's career, and help to keep him in the lifestyle he is accustomed to and wants to maintain.

When Father Time has his way, he can leave the best of us looking older and tired. Nobody can stop the process completely, but the barbering and grooming industry can help put old Father Time in his place and keep the men of today looking younger and feeling good. It's up to you—the barbershop or men's grooming salon owner—to offer the services and products that men want and are willing to buy. The service and retail side of the men's grooming industry is truly booming—right now!

Men want more than just a haircut, buzz cut, and shave; they are looking for the ultimate grooming experience. The barber of yesteryear did not offer, yet alone make serious money from, the service and product sales that are becoming customary in the most successful barbershops.

New Trends in Men's Grooming

- **Beards, Mustaches, and Goatees:** This has become a popular fashion trend and has increasing revenue possibilities. It is not uncommon for movie stars and sport figures to have facial hair, which creates new trends and looks for men of all ages. Barbershops around the world now have another revenue stream when they add and specialize in trimming and styling facial hair.

- **Eyebrow Shaping:** "Guy brows" is a term devised to cater to the rise of men who regularly get their eyebrows professionally waxed. Eyebrow sculpting has really boomed in the last few years. As men age, the extra hair around the eyes makes them look tired and their eyes saggy. By removing and sculpting the hair, it opens up their eyes and gives them a much younger look. Not only does this produce a new revenue stream for your business; but, once they start having this service done, clients tend to continue to have this service done each time they come in for a haircut, which continues producing extra income for your business.

- **Men's Nail Polish:** Nail polish was once something a "real man" would never even think about putting on his hands. But, in today's changing world, men regard manicures and pedicures as an integral part of their grooming process. Actors, sports figures, and muscians have also changed the way men feel about having polish on their nails. If Johnny Depp, Prince Harry, and David Beckham can have their nails done—and not just with clear color, but maybe some other colors as well—why not every other man looking for a new, different, and bold look. Many manufacturers are creating and marketing polish for men, such as BB Couture for Men, AlphaNail and Berardini's Evolution Man.

- **Waxing:** Men are feeling the need to be well-cropped not only on their heads and eyebrows, but all over their bodies. Gone is the caveman look. Chest hair erupting from your collar is no longer considered the "real man" look. A well-cropped man today is considered a man who is successful. It gives them a feeling of masculinity and power. If you are up to it, having waxing services in your men's grooming business can produce a nice revenue stream.

- **Color:** Not too long ago, it was okay for a man to go gray naturally. Going gray gave the man a distinguished look. The experienced man with a lot of business background was like a warrior. The fact that he had gray hair projected the persona to an outsider that this man had done it all successfully. Looking older was expected and that was okay. Well, things have changed. The businessman of today has competition from younger men moving up the ladder quicker. Big companies can hire a much younger person for half the salary of an older person. They can take a chance with a younger person with the hopes that they will blossom into a topnotch employee. The importance of keeping the gray away has never been more important in today's society for the aging man.

- **Skin Care:** Most men do not want to go under the knife for plastic surgery, but are open to facials or and anti-aging creams to reduce the appearance of fine lines and wrinkles. Many big companies are seizing this opportunity to develop and market new products and services to men. With the help of GQ magazine and Men's Health, men are reading about skin care and realizing that it is essential to slowing the aging process. Hiring a good esthetician and offering facials and a skin care line for men is a great revenue stream in for your barbershop.

- **Massage:** Men work and play hard. The idea that massages and spas are only for women is in fact not true. Men have gone to spas dating back to the Roman Empire. Massage was a big part of how the men relaxed after a day of business. Well, today the massage is back. Men want the same spa indulgences that are offered to women. They want to relax after a stressful day at the office. Having a massage therapist at your barbershop can be a great way to earn extra income.

Men fall under the same pressures to be attractive and feel the same enforcement of standards as women. Everybody wants to look their best and stay "younger" longer. The anti-aging craze is bigger than ever and booming. Putting a cap on Father Time is impossible; but, as a barber and professional men's grooming specialist, you have the opportunity to capitalize on these fast growing trends and keep the men that come to your shop in top form and ready to conquer their world.

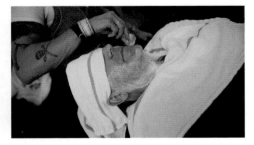

THE GOOD, THE BAD & THE UGLY

(Brought to you by barbershop and salon owners and other industry leaders)

Greg Martin, Owner American Haircuts

"The number one thing that I hear about a good barbershop is, 'Wow, it's so much better here than at my wife's salon.' All of our research indicated that guys don't really care about themes like sports and race cars; they just want their barbershop back. They want a quality cut and a good conversation. Men for the most part base their return to a barber 70% on service and overall experience and conversation, and 30% on the technical quality of the cut."

Sal Immitti, Dukes Barber Shop, Staten Island, New York

"After 35 years in business, I have many loyal customers that give me the respect that I have earned. I have been called many things over the years, barber, stylist, hair guy, mullet guy. Men today want a personal relationship with their barber. They want us to tend to their head, ears, scissors up the nostrils, and dying eyebrows without hesitation. Never once are my customers embarrassed and they feel at home in my barbershop."

CHAPTER 5

Good Barbering Is Not Just About Hair

When opening a new business, you are starting with a clean slate. Call it a fresh start. You may have already thought about employee rules and barbering culture long before opening your new barbershop.

These new business policies are a must for a successful business, but have you thought about guidelines or good barbering business rules for yourself? Good barbering is not just about hair; it's about good business practices that you must follow for business success.

Whether you have been taught to tuck away and save money for a rainy day or not, it is something that you will need to do and start doing from the day you open your doors. If you are reading this book and opening your barbershop is a long-term goal, then start a savings account now. Putting money aside must become a priority for you and your business because it's the unexpected expenses that always seem to arise at the worst possible times.

Next, you will find some financial lessons and workplace truisms that will help you develop money smarts and put you on the financial path for good business growth.

Save With a Purpose

Earmark a portion of your paycheck to set aside for a rainy day fund. Make it a reasonable number you can live with that doesn't affect your standard of living. Normally, 10 percent of your net pay is a good starting point. Whatever the goal, make it concrete and stick to it. As your business grows, you can earmark savings from your profits. In the first year of your business, it is safe to say that most likely this rainy day fund will have to come from your paycheck.

Make It Automatic

Whether you take home a paycheck or cash, make it automatic. Set up an automatic transfer of money from your checking to your savings. If it comes out before you see it, you will not miss it. Before you know it, your rainy day fund will begin to grow. This nest egg can be used for things such as equipment improvements, software upgrades, and marketing. The best part about using savings is that you don't have to borrow from anyone as you make necessary changes in your barbershop.

Start Your Own Tip Jar

The barbering business has always been about tips. You will find that your tip cup may run over quickly as your business grows. This money should be put aside for taxes and business purposes. Using tip money as fun money is not a good practice to follow. Start from the day you open your doors. It's natural to want to use that money to "play," but remember that the IRS wants you to pay on all of your income and that includes tips.

Start a Budget

Budgeting lies at the foundation of every financial plan, whether it's business or personal. It doesn't matter if you're living paycheck to paycheck—know where your money is going if you want a handle on your finances.

Develop a simple budget that you can easily follow. You must know exactly what your monthly expenses are and when bills are due. Put aside the money that is needed each day, week, or month.

This simple budget should track what you have coming in, the portion going into savings, and the amount to cover expenses for your business and personal expenses.

Track Your Spending

The first step in getting your finances to fall within the budget guidelines you set for yourself is to track your spending as much as possible. Not only will you be able to calculate your budgeting guidelines, but you will also know where your money is going, and what adjustments you need to make to get on track and stay out of debt. You should either set this up online or on a paper-based system. This should be done daily so you can quickly react to any overspending and put a quick stop to it by getting yourself back on track.

Try Using Cash to Keep Spending Under Control

Cash is king. If you need something and you have the cash, buy it. If you have to use credit, don't buy it. Swiping credit cards has become too easy. With the ability to use both credit and debit cards to make purchases, you can be in and out of a store and make a purchase without really thinking about what you just bought and the financial impact it may have on your budget and monthly expenses. When you use cash for a purchase, you visibly see what you just spent, how much cash you have left, and the outcome of not having the money for your business or home for the rest of the day, week, or month.

Time Is Money

Time is an entrepreneur's resource because it is the only thing that is truly scarce. Be stingy with it and learn to manage it as best you can. There are only 24 hours in a day, seven days a week, 52 weeks a year, and you must spend time sleeping, eating, relaxing, and of course time with family and friends. Most resources such as how many customers, employees, locations, and products you can have are flexible and can increase or decrease based on your strategy and rate of business success and growth.

Other than self-imposed limits, there are no limits to how much you can make. Remember success doesn't come overnight. It will take many long days and nights, months, and maybe years to build a successful business. Don't want to wear yourself out in the first couple of months. Make sure that you are focusing your energies on aspects of the business that will increase your profitability and always leave time to take care of yourself and your loved ones.

Don't Burn Bridges

You never know who will walk in the door for a haircut. This person can be an attorney, accountant, bank loan officer, police officer and/or a principal of a school. Treat all clients like they are the most important person you will meet in any given day. You will never know if this person can help you with your business as your business grows. Remember the old saying, "It's not what you know; it's who you know that helps you get ahead in life." Treat all your clients with respect and don't ever burn a bridge.

Have you thought about these money-saving ideas?

○ Open a savings account in your business name.

○ Ask your product distributor how you can get discounts.
(Volume buying, perhaps, or when a new product is being introduced.)

○ Put aside money for an emergency.

○ Put aside money for your taxes.

○ Ask your electric company for an energy audit, to see where you could save on electricity costs.

○ Always get multiple quotes for work that you are having done at or for your barbershop.

THE GOOD, THE BAD & THE UGLY

(Brought to you by barbershop and salon owners and other industry leaders)

Mr. Ray's Barbershop

"I learned early on to put away a portion of the barbershop's profits when I could. You never know when Murphy's Law will strike. Trust me, it does; and, you better have the money to fix, repair, and pay your suppliers and taxes. The problem is when you're in business, you never know when the unexpected is coming. You must always be ready!"

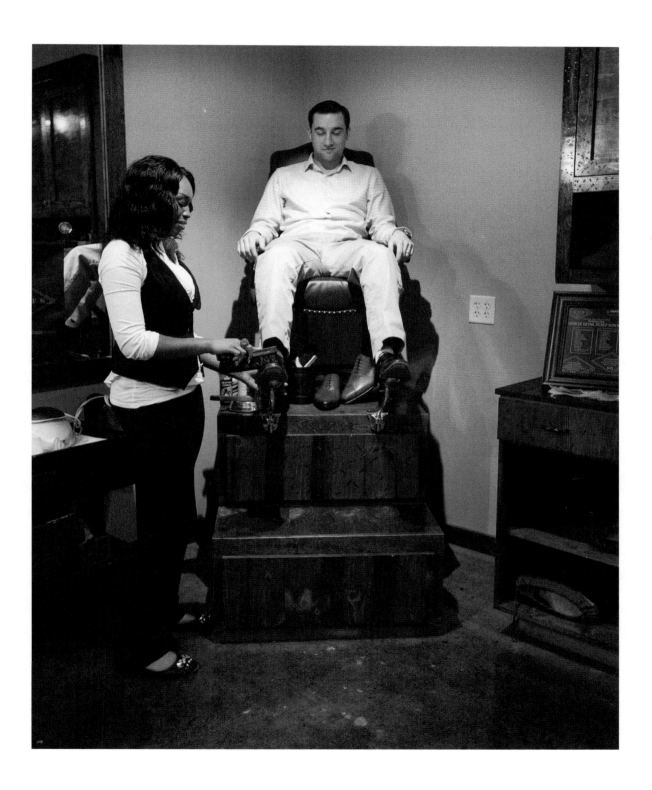

CHAPTER 6

New Business Checklist

"A dream doesn't become reality through magic; it takes sweat, determination, and hard work."

—Colin Powell

Planning is critical when you set out to start your new business. To make sure that you've considered all that's involved, we've collected helpful items for your new business checklist.

You will have to determine how big you want your barbershop to be and the types of services you will offer. A full-service barbershop that includes facials, men's color services, massage therapy, and manicures and pedicures will require more space. A larger space will cost more in rent, along with all the other expenses that go along with it.

The average barbershop in the U.S. is 1,000 square feet. If you add services beyond cutting hair, as described above, you could need as much as 1,800 square feet. Before you invest your time and money blindly, always put your vision on paper.

To get your business vision in order, you will need the following:

- Money or financial backing
- A comprehensive business plan
- Conceptual site plan design and barbershop layout
- Equipment evaluation and supplies
- Budgets, including costs associated with startup, construction, equipment and six months to a year's worth of operating expenses

Breaking down your initial startup costs is also important. The amount of money you will need to get your business up and running is not an easy task to figure out. Consider these factors.

Initial Startup Costs

You will have a better understanding of your startup costs by doing some simple things, such as looking at equipment online, checking out catalogs, going to a local trade show, speaking to a barbershop designer, and calling utility companies for an estimated cost for your space. Speak to potential vendors, accountants, and contractors. All of these things will give you estimates on your monthly overhead and enable you to ensure that the costs are within your budget. All of this should be done before you begin the next step—finding a location. Begin by estimating the expenses you will incur when first opening your business:

- Barber furniture and equipment
- Furniture and equipment for additional services (facials, massage, manicure/pedicure, etc.)
- Office and backroom (tables, chairs, refrigerator, washer/dryer, desks, filing cabinets, etc.)
- Computer system equipment (desktops/laptops/tablets, printers/scanners/fax machines, modem/Internet)
- Signage (outdoor/indoor)
- Phone system (phones and phone lines)
- Sound system
- Lighting
- Display cases
- Reception furniture
- Initial order of products needed for retail, dispensary, and back bar
- Art (pictures, photos, murals, etc.)
- Entertainment (televisions, pool table, foosball table, air hockey table, etc.)
- Bar for complimentary drinks (mugs, glasses)
- Coffee bar
- Deposits for public utilities
- Deposits for your building lease
- Installation of phone and computer lines
- Licenses and permits
- Professional and accounting fees
- First-year premium for business insurance policy

Don't forget construction costs. Construction overruns can be the death of any business startup. The setup and build of any new business will be the most expensive thing you do as a new business owner. Moving into any space may mean changes. Plumbing, electrical, carpentry, flooring, handicap-accessible bathrooms, and air conditioning will be costly and never seem to come in on budget. Always add an extra 20 percent when figuring construction costs; that should cover the unexpected and overruns.

Owner Salary & Payroll

Chances are your startup business will not immediately generate enough revenue to cover all your expenses plus payroll and salary. Therefore, you will need to add your startup costs plus monthly expenses in order to allocate funds for personal expenses.

Depending on your circumstances, and how much money you have put aside for your new business, it could take anywhere from a few months to a year before your business will be able to pay you a salary. If you plan for this, you will not panic after six months when you still don't have enough income to draw a salary. You must always plan conservatively when forecasting salary projections.

Get Organized

This chapter involves breaking down the different parts that are essential for creating a successful business model. By following this guide, it will help you focus on all issues that need to be addressed in the beginning or planning stages.

We suggest you buy a large binder and a set of tabs. You can use them to organize all of your paperwork and ideas for your new client. Create a nice cover for your binder with your barbershop name and logo. This is a motivational and empowering way to get started. Here are the tabs that you need to create for your binder and the types of information that you will start adding to it.

1. Location
2. Business plan
3. Incorporation
4. Financial & Accounting
5. Operational
6. Website
7. Risk Management
8. Revenue
9. Branding/Marketing
10. Furniture & Equipment

Location

1. Print out maps and check out the competition in the area
2. Take pictures
3. Research lease and/or purchase costs
4. Write down or find out contact information for leasing or real estate agent
5. Find at least three locations

Business Plan

1. Create a business plan
2. Capital investment
3. Forecasting, goals, revenue streams
4. Executive Summary

Incorporation

1. Incorporate business
2. Occupational license
3. Create legal business documents, including articles of incorporation
4. Buy-Sell Agreements
5. Open business checking account
6. Agree on partner capital investment
7. Fictitious name registration
8. Obtain business license
9. Obtain EIN (Employment Identification Number)
10. Review all laws for the license and registration requirements

Financial/Accounting

1. Establish payment methods—credit cards, PayPal™, finance options
2. Terms and conditions of payment through suppliers
3. Billing, accounts payable, inventory, software
4. Create detailed financial projections
5. Explore Small Business Administration (SBA) loans, grants, and other available governmental subsidies

Operational

1. Assign duties and responsibilities
2. Number of employees and positions needed
3. Necessary supplies (clippers, capes, combs, brushes, towels, hair dryers, hair products, etc.) needed for budgeting
4. Create relationship with preferred shipper (UPS, FedEx®)
5. Employee training, handbook
6. Payroll program or ADP, a company that provides Automatic Data Processing
7. Hire a bookkeeper/accountant

Website

1. Conceptualize purpose and layout of Web presence
2. Hire Web designer/manager
3. Create domain
4. Email addresses
5. Evaluate and determine ways of marketing on the web, such as Groupon, Facebook, etc.

Risk Management

1. Business insurance
2. Insurance on property and equipment
3. Legal agreements with suppliers
4. Umbrella policy

Revenue

1. Create catalog of merchandise
2. Establish pricing and GM methodology for retail and services

Branding/Marketing

1. Secure the services of a brand expert if you are having trouble coming up with a name and a logo for your barbershop
2. Letterhead and paper supplies, business cards, barbershop menu
3. Set up phones
4. Create an overall marketing strategy and company logos. Be sure to include social media marketing strategies, using tools like Facebook, YouTube, Twitter, Foursquare, Groupon, Google+, and LinkedIn.

Furniture & Equipment

1. Barbershop furniture
2. Barbershop equipment
3. Office equipment & furniture: copiers, computers, networking

THE GOOD, THE BAD & THE UGLY

(Brought to you by barbershop and salon owners and other industry leaders)

Salon, Wilmington, NC

"My mistake was thinking that the construction would only take 30 days, simply because that's what the contractor told me. Then I watched it drag out to 90 (and double in cost) while I went without income!"

"THAT'S WHAT THEY SAY"

"The word 'barber' comes from the Latin word "barba," meaning beard."

Copyright Andrew Dubois 2010

CHAPTER 7

How to Pick the Right Location

"Picking a winning location for your business is like hitting the lotto.
Just like the lotto, you have to make sure you pick a winner!"

—Anonymous

It is said the three most important decisions you will make are location, location, and location. Whether you are creating and building your first barbershop or even relocating or opening a second location, the details of the location might not be the first thing on your mind, but they SHOULD be.

Put location on the top of your list as the single most important factor for your new business. Your amazing concepts, services, and products will go unnoticed if you do not take the time to do your homework and pinpoint the perfect location. Your location is a huge factor in how you market your business, determine which products to carry, and set prices for services. Your location says a lot about you, your shop, and the clients you wish to attract.

Here are several key factors to consider when choosing your barbershop location:

Population & Your Clients

Begin by researching the city and area you have selected for your barbershop thoroughly before making a final decision. Read local papers and speak to the small business owners in the region. Ask them the difficult questions regarding their business: "What unexpected expenses, like taxes and fees, came up when you started your business here? Is the Chamber of Commerce active in promoting new businesses? Is the city or county good at repairing the streets, sidewalks, etc. on which your business is located?"

Obtain location demographics from the library, online, Chamber of Commerce and/or the Census Bureau. The best advice you will receive is from the local coffee shop or restaurants in the neighborhood. Observe the people: how do they dress, where do they shop, when are people shopping, and are they buying.

Accessibility, Visibility, & Traffic

Don't confuse a lot of traffic for a lot of clients. You want your barbershop in a location where there are many shoppers, but only if the shopper meets the definition of your target market. Small retail stores may benefit from the traffic of nearby larger stores. In many cases, the better visibility your shop has, the less advertising needed. A freestanding building on the outskirts of town will need more marketing dollars than the barbershop located in a mall or on a main street. When considering visibility, look at the location from the client's viewpoint and whether you could find the location mixed in with all the other surrounding businesses.

Signage, Zoning, & Planning

Before you enter into a lease or purchase agreement, be sure you understand all the rules, policies, and procedures related to your intended barbershop location. Contact the local city hall and Zoning Commission for information on regulations regarding the space in which you are interested. The planning board determines the correct use for the location. Although the landlord may love the idea of having a full-service barbershop in that location, the planning board will have the final say on whether or not it is allowed.

It also may be a good idea to ask the planning officer about signage and regulations. Many towns are very sensitive about the height and the type of signage allowed.

Competition & Neighbors

When choosing your location, it is a good idea to see how many barbershops are in the same vicinity. Other types of businesses may help or hurt your business. The key is to be next to a retailer that draws other people to the area. Schools, hospitals, and large stores are also a big draw in small towns. Being next to a busy coffee shop or designer store may be fantastic to give you instant exposure. Being next to a muffler shop could be a good thing because of the male clients that will likely come and go from this nearby business. However, a business that is very loud or uses all the available parking could also be a major deterrent. It's important to use the featured "Check It Out" list for your location to weigh the pros and cons.

Location Costs

Besides the base rent, consider all the costs involved when choosing your barbershop location. These costs will be your monthly overhead no matter what else arises:

- Lawn care, snow removal, building maintenance, utilities, and security
- Upkeep and repair of the heating/air conditioning units
- Average utility bill

- Property taxes (depending on the lease)
- Water and sewer costs
- Insurance on the property and contents

Personal Factors

If you are going to be in the barbershop on a daily basis, think about your personal factors. How far is the distance from your home and other things you do on a daily basis? Do you need to take children to school? How close is your bank? How far is shopping? The commute can easily overshadow the exhilaration of your new business if you are spending a lot of time traveling to and from work. Commuting has the potential to stifle your independence.

Questions That Will Make or Break Your Location

Most people focus their energy on the creative side of the new business and neglect some important aspects of choosing a location. Answering these questions for the site you are considering will help you determine if you have chosen the right location for your new business. Following is a list of questions you should answer before choosing your barbershop location.

✓ CHECK IT OUT

Before You Go Any Further

Is the facility located in an area that is zoned for a barbershop?	○ Yes	○ No
Is the facility large enough for your business?	○ Yes	○ No
Does it meet your layout requirements?	○ Yes	○ No

Traffic & Visibility

How many people walk or drive past the location in a given day, week, or month?

Day _____   Week _____   Month _____

Will local businesses attract clients to your barbershop?	○ Yes	○ No
Will there be walk-in business?	○ Yes	○ No
Can you see the location of the barbershop from the main flow of traffic?	○ Yes	○ No
Will the barbershop's sign be visible?	○ Yes	○ No
Is there easy access to the barbershop?	○ Yes	○ No
If the location is off a busy street or highway, is it easy to get to?	○ Yes	○ No

If there is a divider on the main street, would clients have to make a U-turn?	◯ Yes	◯ No
Is this a seasonal community?	◯ Yes	◯ No
Can potential clients see the location at night?	◯ Yes	◯ No

Getting to the Location & Parking

Is the area served by public transportation?	◯ Yes	◯ No
Can clients easily get in and out of the parking lot?	◯ Yes	◯ No
Is there adequate parking?	◯ Yes	◯ No
Does this location have 10 parking spots for every 1,000 square feet of space?	◯ Yes	◯ No

Safety

Is there adequate fire and police presence in the community?	◯ Yes	◯ No
Is there exterior lighting on the building?	◯ Yes	◯ No
Is the surrounding area and parking lot lit up and safe at night?	◯ Yes	◯ No

What is the crime rate in the neighborhood? _____

About the Building

Does the building need repairs?	◯ Yes	◯ No
Does the building have a crawl space or basement for easy access to utilities?	◯ Yes	◯ No
Are the lease terms and rent favorable?	◯ Yes	◯ No

Logistics

Is the location convenient to where you live?	◯ Yes	◯ No
Can you find qualified employees who live in the area?	◯ Yes	◯ No
Can suppliers make deliveries conveniently at this location?	◯ Yes	◯ No

Branding/Marketing/Competition

Does the location have the clients you are looking for?	◯ Yes	◯ No
Does the area have the image you are looking for?	◯ Yes	◯ No
Are there many competitors nearby?	◯ Yes	◯ No

THE GOOD, THE BAD & THE UGLY

(Brought to you by barbershop and salon owners and other industry leaders)

Greg Martin, Owner American Haircuts

"I choose my location based on three primary criteria. I always research the demographics (i.e., the number of households and/or workers in a one to three mile radius). Nothing under 5,000 households within one mile and up to any number combined with workers—the higher the number, the better. One of my locations has 10,000 households within one mile and the other has 35,000. I don't have to tell you which one does more haircuts per month."

Suzanne Thompson Mills

"Not negotiating enough square footage! We have been in the salon for a year and within the first three months had outgrown our space and continue to grow ... other than that, I have no regrets or mistakes that I haven't been able to learn from and turn around to our benefit."

Kim Titu, Pontello

"I started small, wasn't paying for square footage that wasn't producing income. The 1,000 square feet kept it small and cozy until growth required more space. Then moved into a much larger space: too big, too quick, and too expensive."

Nikki Cameron, Salon Owner/Operator

"Not researching the location enough. And I would have interviewed and hired before opening. [It would have been] a lot less headache and given me a little more time to know the staff before working with them."

"THAT'S WHAT THEY SAY"

It's a fact that most barbers work well beyond their retirement age because they love their job and their loyal customers.

James Giordano, USA Barbers, Downtown New York City (Former Trade Center Area)

"The right location was the essential location for us. We catch our clients as they come off the train before work, during their lunch break, and after work."

CHAPTER 8

How to Negotiate Your Lease

"To create something exceptional, your mindset must be relentlessly focused on detail."

—Giorgio Armani

Is this a good time to open your barbershop? Our answer is, "Yes," as long as you find the right location and negotiate a great commercial lease. Since the downturn of the economy, we have seen a huge decrease in commercial shopping center occupancy. Some centers are only 50 percent filled with tenants. Landlords are looking for any opportunity to lease their location and they are giving incredible deals to fill their growing empty spaces.

This creates a huge opportunity that would normally cost you much more. The key is to know what to look for and what questions to ask. Realize that your rent will be one of the largest fixed expenses you have every month.

The importance of negotiating this lease agreement will help you with your budget and financial outlook. Any miscalculations made on the negotiating of this lease will be with you the entire term of the lease. That problem will be very costly and, unfortunately, does not go away once you sign the agreement.

When you are looking for a location for your barbershop, most are available for lease only, not to own or buy. But before you agree to the basic terms of the commercial lease that the landlord hands you, you should realize that there is plenty of leeway in commercial leases for negotiations. Here are the most common facts that will assist you when negotiating your lease. These facts will enable you to negotiate the best deal possible.

- Analyze all costs associated with the potential space (construction, air conditioning, handicap-access bathrooms)
- Is it a triple net or gross lease? Triple net means there are added expenses such as maintenance and property taxes. Gross is a total lease amount with no add-ons.

- City impact fees (example: one-time water hookup with the city)
- Any restriction on services?
- Deposits and down payments
- Free rent

Basic Lease Cost

The first item of business you and your landlord will need to discuss is how much you will pay to rent the space. Usually, your monthly rent will be determined based on the square footage of the space, which is calculated at a per square foot cost. If you take the width and the length, multiply it by the dollars per square feet, and then divide it by 12, that will give you your base monthly rent.

Additional Costs

Sometimes you will have additional costs to figure into your monthly rent expense, called CAM (common area maintenance) or triple net. It is often an addition to the monthly rent or an annual assessment per tenant. The CAM costs include the maintenance of any common areas, like walkways, landscaped places, parking lots, and, in some cases, restrooms.

It is common for the landlord to concede and include CAM charges in the rent price of your commercial lease if negotiated correctly. Getting the most of your leased space is often determined by the market conditions of your location.

Below are some additional CAM expenses to look for when negotiating your lease:

- Property tax
- Snow removal, lawn maintenance, landscaping
- Repairs and maintenance to driveways, sidewalks, or parking lots
- Utilities (electric, gas, sewer, and water)
- Refuse collection
- Security
- Insurance—prorated among tenants
- Structural and roof repairs
- Mechanical system repairs and replacements (such as heating and A/C maintenance and replacement)

> **NOTE**
>
> It is wise not to sign a lease until you are certain that your financing is secure. Otherwise, you may find yourself responsible for lease payments using your own money while you wait for the approval of a loan.

Repairs & Improvements

The repairs and improvements required for the space are a critical part in your lease negotiations. The build-out in a barbershop can be very expensive. If the previous tenant was also a barbershop, changes could be minimal. For many reasons, this is ideal. Here are the three most important factors to look for:

- The amount of electricity coming into the location
- The size of the air conditioner and heating unit
- Handicap-access bathroom requirements

Plumbing, electric, handicap-access bathrooms, lighting, flooring, and painting are all part of the move-in process. Be very cautious when the landlord says "take it as-is." That means you will pay for all repairs and upgrades. If you can do these repairs or improvements yourself, you may be able to do them inexpensively. However, in most cases, the landlord will want a licensed contractor to do the work because of cod requirements for any changes. Some landlords are willing to absorb the cost of reasonable upgrades since you are improving their property.

Financing Your Construction Costs

Obtaining financing from your landlord may be the easiest and the most overlooked method of getting financing. Many landlords have already built money into their financial projections that they will use to attract new tenants. These tenant improvement allowances can range from $5 to $25 per square foot.

The new tenant can use the landlord's contractors to build out the space necessary for the barbershop. The landlord will pay the contractor and reimburse you the monies spent for the build-out once you provide them with documentation. The documentation they are looking for usually includes lien waivers from all contractors/subcontractors and copies of Notice of Occupancy permits from the city/county. Be sure to negotiate the tenant improvements upfront and right into the lease.

Signing Your Life Away—Personal Guaranty

Definition:

- A guarantee that the primary owner will assume personal responsibility for repayment of the loan, should the company not repay the loan.

  www.businesstown.com/finance/money-glossary.asp
- An agreement to make oneself liable or responsible to another for the payment of a debt, default, or performance of a duty by a third party.

  www.crfonline.org/orc/glossary/p.html
- The provision in a lease naming a guarantor who is held personally responsible for the payment of all the amounts for rent and additional rent and other terms as set out in the lease.

  www.gtacommercialrealestate.com/resources.asp

How can you avoid giving a personal guaranty when signing a lease? For almost all new businesses, landlords will want you to sign personally. We recommend signing as a limited liability entity such as a corporation, limited liability, or limited partnership. ***Try to avoid signing a personal guarantee at all costs.***

Tenants ***should not*** grant the landlord a security deposit with an interest in the barbershop furnishings, inventory, and trade fixtures. A security deposit of first and last month's rent payment should suffice.

Buy Out of a Lease—Business Is Over

The tenant should negotiate, upfront, a buyout clause in the lease negotiations. Doing so will allow the tenant of a new business to get out of the lease should the business fail. If the tenant should desire to terminate the lease, the "buyout" clause would be in place. The buyout should provide that the tenant can pay a specific amount of rent, usually from three to six months, to terminate the lease.

Free Rent

It's important in the first year to negotiate a very low rent to allow you to turn a profit quickly or utilize your dollars elsewhere, such as in advertising and marketing. You might be able to negotiate six months free rent in the beginning or half rent. There are so many ways to be creative.

Free rent can be very helpful in the beginning stages of setting up your business—it doesn't matter whether you are opening your first barbershop, relocating your current barbershop, or opening another location. Free rent is free rent and can help offset the costs of your business venture. Here are some reasons why free rent is so important:

- Construction time, including permits, takes 3–4 months; free rent during this building process (no revenue at this point)
- Promoting the barbershop during construction
- Using available money for advertising and marketing
- Bringing staff onto payroll as the barbershop is being built
- Loss of your existing employment while building your new business

Details of Your Commercial Lease Negotiations

Check off the questions below as you get answers.

○ Did you discuss what signage will be acceptable?

○ What happens if you need to relocate?

○ What if an employee wants to buy your business? Can they take over the lease?

○ What happens if you outgrow your space?

○ What happens if you want to downsize?

○ What happens if you go out of business?

Final Steps—Legal Advice

As a final precaution, take the lease to an attorney who specializes in lease agreements. You can never be too careful about signing a commercial lease. Your lawyer will raise any red flags, answer your questions, and explain exactly what you are signing.

THE GOOD, THE BAD & THE UGLY

(Brought to you by barbershop and salon owners and other industry leaders)

Harry Holmann, Creative Hair

"I had an attorney dissect every part of the lease before I would sign anything. No matter how many times I read the lease, my attorney was able to pick up some very important things that I missed that would have cost me a ton of money."

CHAPTER 9

Your Legal Team

"I have no use for body guards, but I have very specific use for a highly trained accountant."

—Elvis Presley

Sometimes, we come across barbershop owners who tried to research and manage all the legal and financial situations on their own. We are here to tell you that the "do it yourself approach" can be a costly mistake. Getting educated on the legal and financial aspects of business and business ownership is always a good idea because it will make it easier to talk to and understand your lawyer, accountant, and bookkeeper. That being said, we are firm believers in learning as much as you can about operating your business. But, don't undervalue or disregard the importance of a good legal and financial team.

From a legal and financial standpoint, each business property lease and business model is different and having the skilled expertise of your lawyer or accountant looking at the finer details will pay off—big time.

Do what you do best—focus on creating the experience for your clients and what will set you apart!

When you put together your legal and financial team, you will want to find professionals who represent small business owners, one of your customers or even other barbershop owners. Lawyers and accountants can be costly, but paying for their services and expertise will save you from the financial losses you could face from poorly negotiated lease agreements, unnecessary lawsuits, late or incorrect tax payments, etc.

Just like everything else in this business venture, you will need to do your research to find the good ones—the ones who will do their best for you. When you need them, you want to know they are there for you and that they understand your business needs! In this chapter, you will find helpful tips about hiring the right lawyer, accountant, and bookkeeper for your business.

Hiring a Lawyer

Having a good business lawyer is essential in negotiating the best lease and properly setting up your business entity. Many aspects of business require legal advice. Once your business is open, you may have issues with other tenants, your landlord, your clients, or your employees that will require the assistance of a lawyer. When a legal problem arises, not having legal representation can put you in a costly position—a position that could have been easily avoided had you secured a lawyer early on in your business venture.

Hiring an attorney and forming a solid business relationship with him or her, can save you money and mitigate risk throughout the course of owning and operating your business.

Here are some examples of why you need a lawyer:

- Signing your business property lease
- Negotiating with the landlord
- Forming your business structure
- Closing on the purchase of real estate
- Closing on the purchase of an existing barbershop
- Litigating any lawsuits

However, if you run into a small problem and you feel it can be handled without the advice of a lawyer, then you can find the right forms or information on legal portals such as AllLaw, found at alllaw.com.

The solution is to have open communication with a lawyer who will be ready to work with you quickly if a situation arises. Get legal advice if you have any questions that will cost you money, whether the legal issue is with your business or personal.

What Kind of Lawyer Do You Need?

Lawyers typically specialize in one type of law or another. You are best off finding a business lawyer who specializes in small businesses. However, a general practice lawyer can handle a wide range of legal matters and may be suited to your business needs.

If a legal matter involves a specialized kind of law like bankruptcy, litigation, taxation, or patent laws, then you need to contact a specialist. Make sure to ask your lawyer whether he or she specializes in a type of law before you decide to hire him or her.

Where Do You Find a Lawyer?

The best way to find a lawyer is through a friend, business acquaintance, or a client referral. You can also use an online directory where information is available about lawyers at their websites. Your state's bar association will also have a referral service that can help put you in touch with a lawyer that best suits your needs. We still say word of mouth and a good old-fashioned phone book are the best methods of finding a lawyer.

Find at least three prospective lawyers. Next, make an appointment and interview the lawyer. Ask questions pertaining to your business needs. The lawyer's answers will give you an indication about whether this lawyer is suitable for you and your business.

Check off the questions below as you ask them.

○ What type of law do you specialize in?

○ Do you have any barbershop owners for clients?

○ What is your experience with negotiating a lease?

○ What are the top three things you look to do for a business owner when negotiating a lease?

○ What experience do you have with employment law?

○ What are your legal fees—are your fees hourly or do you charge a flat rate?

○ Are paralegals or associates available to handle routine matters at lower rates?

○ How long have you been a lawyer and what has been your area of focus?

○ Do you actively write articles or present at seminars for other professionals?

○ What if a matter arises that is outside of your area of expertise?

○ What is your availability to take on new clients and how responsive are you?

How Much Do Lawyers Charge?

Lawyer's fees can sometimes be very expensive. It all depends on what type of legal advice they are giving; and, most importantly, how much time they are spending on your needs. There are many different types of fee arrangements. Most lawyers charge hourly fees. Their fees are calculated by multiplying the amount of hours they spend on your case by an hourly rate.

If a lawyer is reviewing your real estate lease, he may charge you a preset amount or fixed fee. If he or she is filing your articles of incorporation for your new business, he may also charge you a fixed fee. You should always ask a potential lawyer to explain their fees and billing practices. Don't take things for granted. You might think that the lawyer only took a few minutes to help you; and then, later, you receive a bill for a few thousand dollars.

Reading documents, especially the lease for your business, takes more than a few minutes for a lawyer to review. However, a lawyer can save you thousands over the term of your lease when they find and flag loopholes or clauses that are in the favor of your landlord.

Most lawyers require a retainer to get started. In the case of a real estate closing or filing articles of incorporation, the lawyer will send you a bill or you can pay them the day of closing. They usually will have a bill prepared and you will know the detailed breakdown of their fees before the closing.

You also have to remember that you are responsible for court fees, services, or any charges to the lawyer while representing you. This includes the time it takes your lawyer to get to and from the courthouse or legal meetings. Having a good lawyer at hand is one key to having a successful business.

Hiring an Accountant

Just like you need a lawyer to help with the legal matters of your business, you will need an accountant to advise you on the financial aspects of your business. Don't make the mistake of attempting this one on your own.

We tend to think of accountants when it comes to taxes, but there many other services your accountant will provide. Whether you're deciding if you should incorporate your new business or trying to decide whether to buy or lease your barbershop equipment, a good accountant will be able to tell you how such a move would affect your taxes and/or your businesses growth.

You need to make sure that you feel comfortable with the accountant you will be hiring. The accountant should be sincere and trustworthy. If you are clear about your requirements, then you will be able to choose the right accountant.

Your accountant will probably recommend that you also have a bookkeeper to help keep your finances organized and tracked in a timely manner. You can learn QuickBooks and you should be somewhat comfortable with it. However, your time is better spent in other areas— like managing the barbershop and cutting hair.

Having a bookkeeper on your financial team will help you to be better prepared for visits with your accountant and save you money in the long run.

You will find that the daily grind of opening the barbershop, running to the bank, processing credit card payments, scheduling staff, and dealing with all the new personalities is a lot to manage. Having someone else who is responsible for keeping your finances organized is essential. Your bookkeeper should be required to:

- Keep track of checks and other income
- Process credit card balances
- Pay bills and reconcile the business checkbook
- Pay employees as well as file and pay federal and state payroll taxes
- Pay quarterly business taxes
- Keep track of receivables
- Keep track of inventories and commissions to your staff

When choosing your bookkeeper, it is important that you hire an individual who has the same business ethics on how to run your business YOUR WAY with their guidance.

How to Find the Right Accountant

The easiest way to find a good accountant is by asking other business associates who they use for accounting services. You must ask them what type of services their accountant provides; and, most importantly, are they satisfied with the services the accountant offers? If you don't get any worthy referrals using this method, use the Internet to find accountants that are close to where you will open your barbershop. Close proximity to your accountant will make it easier and more manageable for communication and availability.

The Face-to-Face Meeting

Face-to-face meetings are imperative because your accountant is someone you will see throughout the year and this person is going to get to know the most intimate details of your personal and business finances. They will also help you to mold your business for success. You are finding a long-term partner to advise you on the financial matters of your business. It's a big deal. You are establishing a lasting relationship that must be built on trust.

Questions to Ask a Prospective Accountant

- ○ Are you a CPA? (Don't be afraid to ask him or her about their education.)
- ○ Do you work with any other barbershops? If so, how will you avoid conflict?
- ○ If you have worked with barbershops, what type of services did you offer?
- ○ What type of barbershop software programs are you familiar with?
- ○ Will you help grow my business or are you going to be more of a bookkeeper?
- ○ Will you help me set up yearly tax planning?

  They should be able to advise your business so it functions with peak tax efficiency.
- ○ Will you offer personal finance advice?

  A key to a good accountant is not just managing your business, but also managing your personal finance as well. Both must be managed correctly, for you to succeed.
- ○ Does this accounting firm have the state-of-the-art technology needed and software to enable me to work and communicate with you efficiently? Describe it.

  Technology has improved small business capabilities. Good communications is vital with your accountant, and the internet has made that easy.

○ Is the accountant you interview a leader and/or a powerful figure in your community?

○ What organizations do you belong to?

○ Are you affiliated with a local bank?

(You may never know when you need a loan). Don't look at your new accountant as a bookkeeper. Ask them if they have the ability to refer business to your new barbershop.

○ What type of business advice would you give me right now, before I open, which could help save me money? The question will give you a good idea if this person is right for you.

○ Why should I hire you? The answer they give will paint a clear picture if they fit in your business plan.

THE GOOD, THE BAD & THE UGLY

(Brought to you by barbershop and salon owners and other industry leaders)

Dawn Brown Garrett

"My mistake was my choice of a business partner and attorney."

Nancy Williams, Raise Your Hair

"I tried to manage without an accountant and bookkeeper. I really have no experience in bookkeeping. Within six months of opening my salon, I was behind on my taxes. I hired an accountant that a client recommended and she saved my business. It was the best thing I ever did. I don't know what I would do without her."

Suzy Tryall, Noel's House of Color, Denver, CO

"Can't live without my accountant! Good ones are out there; you just have to find the ones who are honest and never cheat ... doing what's legal and fair."

American Haircuts, Wallace Barlow, Director of Education, Global Educator/Platform Artist for Woody's Quality Grooming, Educator/Platform Artist for The Andis Company

"Not sure you need to hire an attorney, full time, but certainly consult and listen to their advice or expertise on all important business decisions."

CHAPTER 10

Choosing a Business Structure

"Corporation: an ingenious device for obtaining profits without individual responsibility."

—Ambrose Bierce

New barbershop owners need to have an understanding and make a choice of how they want to legally set up their business. Even existing barbershop owners need to revisit their business structure because there are several choices when it comes to the types of legal organizational structures. The type of business structure you decide upon will affect how much you pay in taxes, the amount of paperwork your business is required to do, the personal liability you face, and your ability to borrow money. An accountant or a lawyer can assist you with the choice that would be best for you and the success of your business.

The business structure you choose will lay down the foundation you need to conduct a legal business enterprise and will also protect you in case you or one of your employees causes an accident and/or damages to one of your clients or your landlord's property. If a lawsuit arises from the accident, your home, business, and assets could be at risk if not properly protected. The legal structure you select should protect you in these cases. However, many first-time barbershop owners often overlook or ignore the ability to choose the business structure that will give them the greatest protection.

Sole Proprietorship

A sole proprietorship is the simplest and most straightforward form of business organization. It is easy to form and offers complete control to the owner. It is an unincorporated business owned entirely by one individual and does not require massive amounts of complicated tax forms.

A barbershop owner who operates with no other employees besides themselves usually chooses a sole proprietorship. This can be a home-based business or operate out of a retail commercial location. In general, the owner is also personally liable for all financial obligations and debts of the business.

Every sole proprietor is required to keep sufficient records to comply with federal tax requirements regarding business documents. They do not have taxes withheld from their business income; they will need to make quarterly estimated tax payments. These estimated payments include both income tax and self-employment taxes for Social Security and Medicare.

One advantage of the sole proprietorship is that additional expenses, such as office expenses, property taxes, utilities, and vehicle expenses may be deducted from the proprietor's income on their taxes.

The liability of a sole proprietorship is the full responsibility for any debt and liability and lawsuit that the company might incur. It means that the individual barbershop owner is held personally responsible for damages, problems, or adverse consequences resulting from the operation of the business.

Partnership

A partnership is the relationship existing between two or more persons who join each other to carry on a business with one goal—to earn a profit. Each person contributes money, property, labor, or skill and expects to share in the profits and losses of the business.

It is usually assumed, under most states' laws, that all partners will share control over the business equally. You can state in the partnership agreement which partners are responsible for the job description to which they agree. You may also want to establish voting rights based on the percentage of the initial investment or how the amount of work and hours will be distributed amongst each partner. Your agreement should spell all of this out prior to opening the barbershop.

In addition, you can specify in your partnership agreement how profits, losses, and salaries will be allocated among partners. It is also based on initial investment and time put into the business. If everyone is equal and puts in the same investment, this agreement becomes very easy.

A partnership agreement should also address the eventuality of a partner leaving the business, a partner who is no longer capable of working in the barbershop, the death of a partner, and the addition of new partners.

Partnership Taxation

Like a sole proprietorship, a partnership has one level of taxation. A partnership is a tax-reporting entity, not a tax-paying entity, which means that profits pass through the partnership to the owners and are divided in accordance with what was agreed to and specified in the partnership agreement. There are no restrictions on how profits are allocated among partners as long as there is economic reason. The partners are responsible for good bookkeeping, paying their tax obligation, Social Security, and Medicaid.

Liability

While there are many benefits of a partnership, one disadvantage is that the owners have unlimited personal liability for their own actions and the actions of their partners. In general, each partner in the barbershop is jointly liable for the partnership obligations. Joint liability means that the partners can be sued as a group. In some states, each partner can be held accountable for the damages from the wrongdoing of other partners and for the debts and obligations of the partnership. Three rules for liability in a partnership are:

- Every partner is liable for his or her actions.
- Every partner is liable for the actions of the other partners.
- Every partner is liable for the actions of the employees of the business.

Corporation

There are many reasons to form a corporation to conduct business. Many entrepreneurs aren't comfortable remaining in a sole proprietorship and require a level of protection not afforded by a sole proprietorship. While some owners think incorporating is only for big companies, the most common form of a business now is to own and operate a business as a corporation.

A corporation is commonly referred to as a limited company or just "company." Some of the main advantages of using a corporation to conduct business include the following:

- **Limited Liability**: The owners of the corporation are shareholders in the business and are not liable for the debts and obligations of the corporation. Creditors cannot hold the shareholders responsible for the debts of the corporation. If the company cannot pay its debt, the creditors cannot go after the shareholders personally. This is one of the main reasons people form a corporation.

- **Ownership Easily Transferable**: Ownership of a corporation is transferred easily by transferring the shares. It can be as simple as endorsing the back of the share certificate.

- **Tax Advantages**: If a corporation operates as a small business and has active income, then it can take advantages of small business deductions and pay income taxes at a substantially reduced rate. There can be a significant tax savings compared to doing business outside of a corporation. A corporation files a separate income tax return. If a shareholder is an employee, he pays income tax on his wages, and the corporation and the employee each pay one-half of the Social Security and Medicare taxes and the corporation can deduct half. A corporate shareholder only pays income tax for any dividends received.

- **Raising Capital**: It is easier to raise capital for a corporation than it is for a partnership or sole proprietor. Lenders are more willing to lend capital to a corporation.

Limited Liability/LLC

A limited liability corporation, also known as an LLC, is a relatively new legal business definition which was formed specifically to provide a host of benefits to new business owners not offered by other entities.

Liability Benefits

One of the biggest benefits of an LLC is that all owners of a limited liability company are protected from being personally liable for the debts, obligations, and lawsuits of the LLC. The LLC benefit states that a member is not liable just because he or she is a member/owner of the LLC. There are guidelines that need to be followed by the principals and/or the members of the LLC so this protection is not lost.

Informal Decision Making

In an LLC, the owners determine the ownership structure, the right to the profits, voting rights, and any other aspect of relationships amongst members. An LLC does not require a board of directors, shareholder meetings, and other managerial formalities, which allow the owners to focus more on their business and less on the requirements and maintenance of corporate guidelines and mandates.

Flexible Tax Choices

The tax choices for an LLC are the second biggest benefit of an LLC for small business owners. The single-member LLC (owned by an individual) can take advantage of having simple sole proprietorship federal income taxation, but without the personal liability of the sole proprietorship.

What does that mean? As a barbershop owner, you are able to write off all the expenses of a home office, utilities, and car. Usually, you would normally not have the benefit of doing so. Both a single and multimember LLC can choose to be taxed as a corporation as well. The tax benefits of an LLC provide more choices than other legal entities.

When you finally do decide which legal structure is right for your business, it's important to choose the entity that gives you the most protection from personal liability with the best tax advantages for your specific situation.

Given all the benefits and flexibility to business owners, business people, lawyers, and accountants now consider the limited liability corporation as the presumptive choice for new business. However, only a good numbers person can look at your current situation and long-term goals to give you the kind of sound objective counsel you need to make the best decision. A good CPA may cost you some upfront money; but, in the long run, it will be money well spent.

"THAT'S WHAT THEY SAY"

"The modern barber pole originated in the days when bloodletting was one of the principal duties of the barber. The two spiral ribbons painted around the pole represent the two long bandages: one twisted around the arm before bleeding, and the other used to bind it afterward. Originally, when not in use, the pole had the bandages wound around it so that both might be together when needed, was hung at the door as a sign. But later, for convenience, instead of hanging out the original pole, another one was painted in imitation of it and given a permanent place on the outside of the shop. This was the beginning of the modern barber pole."

(Source: barberpole.com)

CHAPTER 11

Setting Up Your Business Checking Account

Opening a business checking account is one of the first of many things you will be doing when starting your new barbershop. It is a necessity for corporations and limited liability corporations (LLCs). The opening of a business account will eliminate the commingling of business and personal funds. Keeping business funds separate helps you keep track of transactions made in your business, maintain good records for tax time, and monitor the financial health of your business.

Many new and existing barbershops have three separate checking accounts. They use one for paying bills, another for payroll, and one for credit card processing. It is important that you choose a bank that is in close proximity to your barbershop or your home. Doing so will allow you to develop a personal relationship when you stop into your bank with deposits or any other issues you may have in the course of your daily business operation.

Business owners should research the different business accounts offered at various banking institutions to determine which business account best suits the needs of their business. You can open a business bank account through a bank or credit union. Many will allow you to start the account application process in person, by phone, or online. We feel that a one-on-one meeting with your new banker is the best way to establish a new business relationship with your bank. Your banker will be one of the most important people you do business with on a daily basis.

When trying to figure out what bank best suits your needs, it may pay to start with the financial institution where you currently have your personal account. Since you already have a relationship established, you can easily ask them what type of business programs they have.

✓ CHECK IT OUT

Which Bank Is Right for You?

- ○ Close proximity to work or home for convenience of making daily deposits
- ○ Free check writing
- ○ Lower business processing fees
- ○ Better interest rates on a loan based on the deposits you bring in daily
- ○ Free debit cards
- ○ Online banking and bill paying
- ○ Fee structure for all business transactions
- ○ Interest earned on daily monies in your business checking account
- ○ Business savings account
- ○ Willingness to consider giving you a loan for future growth or expansion
- ○ Understanding of the beauty and men's grooming industry (Do they have any barbershops as clients?)
- ○ Free ATM transactions
- ○ What type of balances do you have to maintain to keep your business checking account open? (Knowing this information when you open your account will help you avoid fees.)
- ○ Free business checks
- ○ Overdraft protection on your account
- ○ No fees for bounced checks

Once you have determined the bank that works best for your business, you will need to open your account. Check with your new banker in regards to what items they require when opening your account; each bank is different. Paperwork will depend upon your type of business ownership and what type of business accounts you want to open. Generally, you will need the items listed below:

EIN-Employer Identification Number

Every corporation, partnership, or LLC must present its Employer Identification Number to obtain a business bank account. Your EIN number is a nine-digit number used to identify the company for banking and taxation purposes. Your

EIN number will show your legal name and the owners of the company and the shares they own. Sole proprietors who do not have an EIN will be required to use their Social Security Number to open a business checking account.

Articles of Incorporation

A new business needs to present its formation documents to establish a business account. Corporation (INCs) must present articles of incorporation, while Limited Liability Corporations (LLCs) must present articles of organization to open a business bank account. Partnership businesses must present a copy of the company's partnership agreement to verify the existence of the company.

Businesses that operate as a sole proprietorship will be required to submit the name filing or trade name certificate to the bank. Sole proprietors who have chosen to use the legal name of the business owner are not required to submit a trade name certificate. They may only need a business license when opening the new account.

Resolution

A resolution must be submitted to the bank to identify the individuals who are authorized to use the business bank account. The resolution should include the name, address, Social Security Number, and position of each person authorized to use the company's account. Sole proprietors do not require a resolution; usually the business owner is the only person authorized to use the account, unless a manager or bookkeeper is requested to do so. In a partnership, each partner may have equal access to use the company's business bank account.

Identification

The people identified in the corporate resolution must bring the appropriate identification to establish a business bank account. Driver's license, Social Security card, birth certificate, and/or passport will be necessary when you open the account.

Initial Deposit

Most banks require a small deposit to open a business account, but a larger deposit is a smart move to avoid those unpleasant bank service charges. You can open a business account for only $25 at most banks around the country.

✓ CHECK IT OUT

Check off the items below as you obtain or gather them:

- ◯ EIN—Employer Identification Number
- ◯ Articles of Incorporation
- ◯ Resolution
- ◯ Identification
- ◯ Initial Deposit

THE GOOD, THE BAD & THE UGLY

(Brought to you by barbershop and salon owners and other industry leaders)

Ricky's Barber Shops, Annapolis Maryland

"From the first day I opened, I used my banker as a sounding board. We discussed business opportunities and growth. Through my bank, I was able to open up my second, third, and fourth locations. Make your banker your best friend!!"

CHAPTER 12

Licenses & Permits to Start Your Business

Starting your barbershop business is going to require a "To Do List" a mile long. Many tasks need to be completed before you even think about opening your doors for business, including adherence to state requirements. You will need to obtain a number of licenses and permits from federal, state, and local governments. Every city and state has different laws and requirements when starting a new business.

The process can sometimes be long and confusing. Start filling out the paperwork as soon as you can, expect delays, and provide all the information necessary to avoid any problems with the opening of your business. For the most part, the different requirements are all variations of a few basic elements. Keeping this in mind, we have listed below the different types of licenses and permits you may need to acquire prior to opening for business.

Business Operation License

When operating a barbershop and selling retail, you will be required to have a basic business operation license from the city or from the local county. The process for gaining a license will be different in each city or state, but will require an application fee, the name of the owner, name of the company, nature of the business, and where the owner plans to operate. Make sure your application is accepted and you meet all of their requirements. You will not be able to open your doors without this.

- Your state website has all state applications online
- Your local municipality has all local applications available

Certificate of Occupancy

Most local governments will require a Certificate of Occupancy, issued by the building department. The certificate is to ensure that you comply with applicable building codes and other laws, and indicates your building to be in a condition suitable for occupancy. The Certificate of Occupancy is also necessary to close on a mortgage if you constructed a building for your barbershop.

License to Sell Retail

Many states require you to have a license to sell different types of retail products. In the barbershop business, you will be selling mainly haircare products. Your town may not require any specific license for this.

Federal Employer Identification Number (EIN)

If the state in which you operate has state income tax, you will have to register and obtain an Employer Identification Number (EIN) from your State Department of Revenue or Treasury Department. For more information, go to www.irs.gov.

Fire Department Permit

Most of the time, this permit is a town requirement and requires that an annual fee be paid. A fire safety person will come to your location before the barbershop opens to make sure you have met the fire department's safety requirements. The requirements are smoke detectors, proper fire exits and signage, and fire extinguishers.

Building Permits

If you plan on doing any extensive remodeling of the space you will occupy or make any changes, your town may require electrical or plumbing permits. The requirements and permits will always fall back on the occupant of the space, but your contractor should take care of these permits and make sure they are filed with the town, inspected and met without any contingencies.

Cosmetology License/Barber License

It is illegal to practice cosmetology or barbering without a valid license. It will be your responsibility as an owner to make sure you and your employees meet the state guidelines with continuing education to keep your license valid. The state will send an inspector to your barbershop to review each of your employees' licenses to make sure they are current and visibly displayed.

Check off the permits below as you obtain them.

○ Business Operation License
○ Certificate of Occupancy
○ License to Sell Retail
○ Federal Employer Identification Number
○ Seller's Permit
○ Fire Department Permit
○ Building Permits
○ Barber/Cosmetology Licenses

"THAT'S WHAT THEY SAY"

Almost the entire barber shop population got lost, due to the popularity of unisex salons in the early 1970's. Long hair was in and the flat top was out!

CHAPTER 13

The Distinctive Barbershop

"Cave: a natural passage under or in the earth where one can seek shelter."

"A Man Cave: a dedicated area such as a garage, basement, or workshop where a man can seek shelter from his wife and family to be alone or socialize with his friends."

—Anonymous

What makes your barbershop different than others in your area is up to you. We all think we have the best ideas when it comes to being unique. The fact is most ideas have been done already. Yes, being the best barber in town and having a great staff is very important, but how you market the barbershop, attract new clients, and keep them coming back are the most important things to having a successful barbershop business.

So, how do you create the experience and the environment that men are men looking for? They are looking for a place that combines the community and nostalgia of an old barbershop, outstanding customer service, professionalism, and a 1920s country club vibe. These grooming locations should have a masculine feel where a man can relax, unwind, and confidently enjoy the highest quality haircut, shave, or spa service in town.

One of the first things you must explore is what you can do to provide standout service that keeps your clients happy and coming back, yet doesn't cost too much. As your business grows, you will be able to spend more on other ideas and marketing that will be a bit more expensive to put in place.

Simple & Inexpensive Ways to Keep Clients Happy

- Welcome clients when they come into your shop.
- Provide different types of magazines for your clients. Suggestions: video game

magazines for the younger clients, popular magazines such as Sports Illustrated, Men's Health, and Cigar Aficionado in your waiting area for general clients.

- Remember important facts that you spoke to your client about the last time they visited. Pick up where you left off.

- Know what cut your client wants and is accustomed to without having to ask them.

- Thank them for their business when they leave.

- Offer a beverage: coffee, soda, or bottled water while they are waiting or having their service done.

- Have a relaxing waiting area for your clients to read or hang out while they wait to have their haircut or wait for their son or friend to finish with their service.

- Make popcorn, either in a microwave or with a dedicated machine.

- Have an espresso machine or coffee bar.

The barbershop of yesteryear is still around, but the simple shop with a few old-style barber chairs has evolved into more of a hip, men's grooming spot. The business has become the meeting place of the community for teenagers and men looking to relax, kick back and share stories, watch a sporting event; or, in some cases, play a game of pool or cards. And, most importantly, get their haircut and maybe a shave.

Standout Ideas for Your Barbershop

Here is a list of things that you can incorporate into your place of business that will make you stand out.

- ◯ Pool table, if you have enough room and space.

- ◯ Old style juke box. Looks sharp and will be a nice attraction to your barbershop.

- ◯ Fish tank. The bigger the better, if you have the room. This is a great centerpiece. Kids love it and it gives a cool, relaxing vibe to your barbershop. Just remember that it will require maintenance. A service you can pay for or do on your own.

- ◯ Shoeshine station. If you have it and can fit it in, you must have someone available to shine shoes. Perhaps you could offer shines on specific days of the week.

- ◯ Large bulletin board. This should allow people to post events and business services they offer.

- ◯ Sports memorabilia area or theme. Guys love sports and local teams. If you're in New York, then the Yankees, Mets, Giants, and Jets merchandise should be displayed around your shop.

○ High school sports pictures would make local teens feel proud when they come in the shop. Having the ability to change the clippings weekly is a nice touch.

○ Old phone booth. I know people don't use coin phones these days; but for someone looking to have a private conversation, this is a slick way to offer that. Yes, it takes up space; but if you can find it, it will be the centerpiece of your shop and a nice conversation piece.

○ Waiting area. This area needs to be inviting and comfortable and have enough space for your clients to stretch out and relax.

○ Flat screen television. These should be placed around the barbershop to offer your clients the ability to watch television.

○ Computer area. Your clients can connect with work or family while visiting your shop. If you don't have the space for a computer work area, you can let them use a company laptop or iPad. If money is an issue, then at least offer free Wi-Fi.

○ Gaming is cool and kids love it. If you have the space, offer a designated area for gaming while the kids wait to get their haircut or are waiting for their parent to finish with their service.

The Guy Style

When choosing furniture and trying to come up with a different look, feel, or vibe in your barbershop, you have to think about what fits your clients. Young, married businessmen and sports types all like different barbershop atmosphere. Trying to make your barbershop fit everyone's personality will be impossible. It comes down to what you think will make your clients happy and will give them an overall atmosphere that fits their wants and needs for the ultimate barbering experience.

Some men like to exist in a cave-like atmosphere (a.k.a., man cave) with no more than a big burly chair and a giant flat-screen TV. For others, furniture, like nice big leather couches and mahogany, may be a way for them to feel masculine and express their success. When you bring these same things into your barbershop, you are reflecting an image with which they want to be associated with. If you are opening your barbershop in a progressive urban area, where upbeat, contemporary style would be appreciated, then find ways to accomplish it by, bringing in old furniture pieces or barber signs, barber poles, and the like to create a refurbished, eclectic feel.

Every Guy's Sofas

While there are many terrific black leather sofas on the market, the poster child of testosterone isn't the only choice for masculine style. Look for a sofa with a rugged look with "bomber jacket brown" upholstery or a denim jean look. You may go with a sleek chrome-leg design. Don't be afraid of country. Plaids are true Old West rustic cowboy, "real man" colors.

Size Matters

No matter what type of furniture you pick, guys like big. In fact, the bigger, the better. Look for deep seats and real wide cushions on your reception furniture and barber chairs. If you plan on having a sports theme, make sure the upholstery is tough enough for guys to tackle the chair or each other while watching a sporting event.

Keep It Down

Inside your barbershop/men's grooming room, you will need to pump up the volume. You must invest in a nice sound system. To reduce neighbor complaints and enjoy better sound quality, you may want to invest in good acoustical ceiling panels when building out your space.

Men's Club or Man Cave

From tree houses to men's clubs, most guys want a place they can escape to and a place they can call their own. The boy's club theme has been around for centuries. There are many ways that you can accomplish this look and feel for your barbershop. Go with your gut and have fun with your planning.

When designing your barbershop, did you think about:

- ◯ Separating areas based on different interests: sports, weather, Wall Street, fashion, movie lovers, car lovers
- ◯ Adding pictures of sports figures or popular older movies: Rocky, Jaws, to name a few
- ◯ Neon signs
- ◯ Bar nicely done with classic beer steins
- ◯ Baseball or football theme
- ◯ Nothing like old-time boxing posters to decorate your barbershop

THE GOOD, THE BAD & THE UGLY

(Brought to you by barbershop and salon owners and other industry leaders)

Mr. Ray's Barbershop, Tampa, Florida

"I opened up my second barbershop. This shop was in a high-end area. My clientele are successful men, more of the 'metrosexual' type. I had to offer more than the traditional barbershop atmosphere. I went with high-end furniture, deep rich colors in the salon with more of an upscale look."

American Haircuts, Wallace Barlow, Director of Education, Global Educator/Platform Artist for Woody's Quality Grooming, Educator/Platform Artist for The Andis Company

"I honestly feel that guys enjoy the high-end men's barbershop or 'Man Cave' environment based on the fact that men can be 'MEN'—a no frills place where they can crack jokes, have a scotch or bourbon, and relax while getting a great haircut. It's also like being part of a country club without the dues. In fact, the American Haircuts concept was voted 'Best in Atlanta' two years in a row."

"THAT'S WHAT THEY SAY"

"No people were better patrons of the barbers than the Romans. They often devoted several hours each day, which included shaving, haircutting, hairdressing, massaging, manicuring, and the application of rare ointments and cosmetics of unknown formulas."

CHAPTER 14

Designing & Space-Planning for Your Barbershop

"Great opportunity is related to great design; you rarely get one without the other."

—Giorgio Armani

Once you have picked your location and signed the lease, it's time to plan your space. In most shopping centers, you'll find that the spaces available are rectangular with the following dimensions:

- 20' x 60' or 1,200 square feet
- 20' x 70' or 1,400 square feet
- 20' x 80' or 1,600 square feet

In this chapter, we will dissect each department, talk about the different types of furniture to use, and the ways to make each area efficient and productive.

When walking into your barbershop, the most important thing is the client's first impression or the "WOW" factor. The experience sets the tone in someone's mind about the shop. It is very important to give an excellent "first impression."

The Entrance & Waiting Area

When the client initially walks in through the front door, it is important that their eyes have a focal point on retail and a person to go to for immediate direction. However, this can be accomplished with or without a front desk.

Many traditional barbershops don't have a front desk. Clients are usually greeted by the owner who is at or near his station, which is closest to the door of the barbershop. He is the front person, the "gatekeeper." However, today's business model is changing the traditional set up. Now, there is more emphasis on retail and a front desk, creating prominence and dedicating an area for retail introduces another revenue stream for barbershop owners.

For an old school barbershop feel, a front desk may not fit with the experience you are trying to create. Even a hip and trendy community-centric shop may forgo the front desk and rely on their super friendly staff to say hello and welcome new guests as they arrive. On the other hand, if you are running a high-class barbershop that gives clients an exclusive, member's only type of feeling, then a front desk and formal reception area is a great way to create this environment and feeling.

For barbershops that will have a reception and front desk area as part of the overall design concept, you should focus on choosing a desk that is both functional and pleasing to the eye, because that's one of the first things your client sees.

The front desk is your control center—we recommend a masculine feel for a great first impression. Every barbershop location and setup is different. Most reception desks contain a place for one or two phones, a computer, a keyboard, a printer, and a writing shelf for the client. When designing your desk, keep functional space in mind and make the size big enough to manage your operation properly. The size of the desk is a big variable, depending on the size of the barbershop and the amount of staff. In a large barbershop, you might have a "check-in desk" for arriving clients and a separate "checkout desk" for making service payments and scheduling future appointments. When designing your barbershop, your front desk must be designed to handle a lot of different functions, which include:

- Booking appointments
- Answering the phone
- Greeting clients
- Collecting for services rendered
- Selling other services and products
- Getting clients' email address for scheduling appointments and reminder notices
- All accounting for daily work
- Updating client information
- Offering beverages

Going without a front desk? Use the extra room to create an inviting reception area with large, oversized chairs or couches and be sure to maximize the retail space, which we will cover next.

Retail & Seating

Above, we indicated standard sizes of a barbershop. For these dimensions, the retail/reception spot should be 200 to 300 square feet. So, if a barbershop is 20 feet wide, then your area is 10–15 feet deep. Doing so will give you room to put in an ample amount of retail space and seating for your clients.

In most traditional barbershops, it is not uncommon to have a very basic waiting chair because it was "first come first serve" with no appointments necessary. The idea was to get you in and out. In the new era of barbering, the traditional waiting area has evolved into a space that is made for gathering and hanging out. In this new space, clients may watch a sporting event, sit back and read a magazine, or sip a fine scotch while listening to some cool jazz. Couches, big leather chairs, and futons are more common in barbershops all around the country today.

The amount of reception chairs depends on the size of your location, the amount of barbers you have and the services you offer. Here are some rules of thumb for seating:

- 4 barber stations, 3 reception chairs
- 6 barber stations, 4 reception chairs
- 8 barber stations, 5 reception chairs
- 10 barber stations, 7 reception chairs
- 12 barber stations, 8 reception chairs

That being said, if your barbershop style is a no appointment necessary, casual community environment, you can mix it up and have different "seating areas." You might have a pool table or foosball table so that people can play while they wait. Or, you might want a coffee/liquor bar where you can serve a complimentary drink to a client who is waiting for their service. Another idea would be a gaming and/or working area; be sure to offer free Wi-Fi to your clients. Retail should be available at and around all of these "seating/waiting" zones.

Retail displays are extremely important because this brings in additional revenue to your business. Depending on your location, retail displays should be properly lighted to illustrate the product.

Make retail a priority when designing your location. This consideration has the most upside potential to create a retail revenue stream. We highly recommend utilizing a lot of space for retail. Call your local distributor to find out what type of retail units come with the product you will be purchasing. Leave at least 5' of wall space in the reception area on both sides for wall displays. For freestanding displays, choose a style that fits into your design without compromising the flow of your barbershop. If you have the space, you should set up the zone like a "store within your barbershop." It has a lot of appeal and gives the client the impression of a professional atmosphere. Here is a typical design for the front of a barbershop:

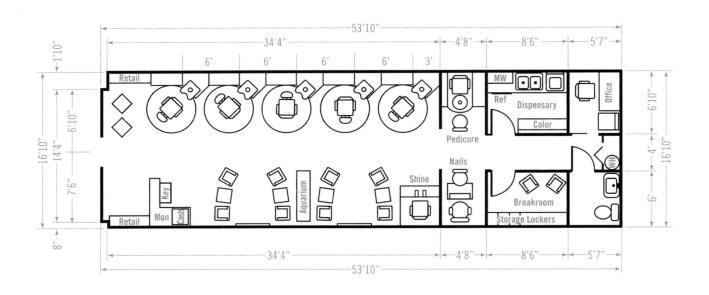

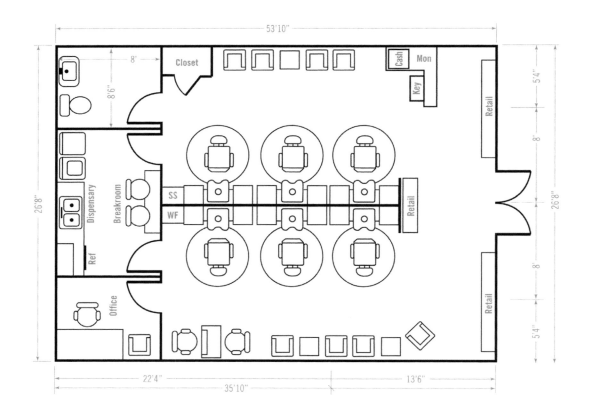

The Barbering Area

The barbering area is where your clients will spend the most time. Setting it up for your clients' comfort and yours is very important. Men who are getting haircuts prefer to socialize with not only their barber, but the other barbers and other patrons. However, if you offer hair coloring services, then you should consider having color rooms or a section of the barbershop with taller walls and maybe curtains for privacy. Most men prefer not to be seen for hair color services. Hair coloring is a new revenue streams for barbershops today, and changes the traditional style of the open atmosphere barbershop.

So, how do you figure out the space requirements for the main floor of the barbering area where all the haircutting takes place? The minimum space for a wall station, from center-to-center of each station, is 6 feet. It gives just enough room for each barber to work and does not waste any space.

Freestanding Stations

They should be no wider than 36 inches and as narrow as possible. Most of the storage space needs to be located on the sides of the units with a small shelf in front, where the mirror is located. When discussing space planning, the unit is normally 36 inches wide and 30–36 inches deep. If you add chairs on each side, the unit takes up 12 feet of depth.

One thing that needs to be considered, when discussing a freestanding unit, is the walkway space around the unit where the barber is working. This is usually a main traffic area. So, it is recommended that another 3 feet is added to each side for the flow of traffic. The overall depth of the station, including traffic, is 18 feet. It can change by the way you might angle the station, but you won't know until you space-plan the complete barbershop.

Be aware that you need to hook electrical to the freestanding station, which will either come from the floor or the ceiling. Either one can be expensive and must be researched while designing. Potential added expenses for freestanding shampoo unit:

- Concrete floor, no basement: you will need to cut the concrete to run wiring
- Exposed wires from the ceiling: unattractive and may not get proper electrical approval
- Increased electrical panel expense: upgrading the service
- Additional lighting: need more light

Here are some general dimensions for laying out your barbering stations:

Wall Mounted Barbering Area

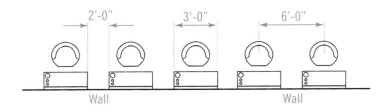

Freestanding Barbering Area

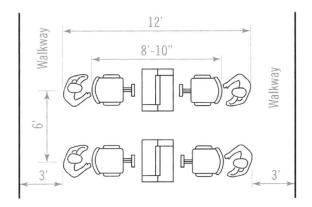

Barber Chair Design

Different chair styles:

1. Chair containing round or five-star, heavy-bottom base: The overall dimensions are approximately 30 inches by 30 inches around. Weight varies from chair to chair. A good quality chair usually weighs 125 pounds or more.

   a. Round base: more stability, with weight and diameter a factor. For cleaning, it is recommended that the chairs are moveable because a ring develops around the bottom of the base from hair buildup.

   b. 5-star base: It is very difficult to find a "true" authentic barber chair with a 5-star base. There isn't much stability with a 5-star base with the heavy chair top. If you insist on this type of bottom, there are some companies that will accommodate this request. This style is easier to clean by taking a hair blower and blowing out all the hair that builds up underneath the chair. But, the lack of stability makes the 5-star base a poor choice for a barbershop.

2. Chair with a U-shaped, T-shaped, or platform footrest:

   a. U-shaped: this is a footrest shaped like a U and has been in the industry for many years. Clients tend to trip over it when getting off the chair.

b. T-shaped footrest: this footrest was developed about 30 years ago, originally in Europe. It is found to be a much better design for clients.

c. Platform: This footrest is widely used for barber chairs. The design allows people to rest both feet completely on the footrest without any overhang. NOTE: Do not allow your client to step off the footrest before you let the chair all the way down in the lowest height position. Otherwise, the chair could tip over and cause an injury.

3. Barber chair with no footrest:

Note: this does not apply to a barber chair. If you find a barber chair that has no footrest, it's probably missing and we would not recommend buying it.

Cleaning & Maintenance

All your equipment needs to be cleaned and many people do not know what type of cleaner to use. Ninety-nine percent of all chairs manufactured these days are made of vinyl, which is a soft, expandable plastic material. Many chairs have buildup from styling products and use. Owners do not know how to clean them properly. The best product is mineral spirits, which has an oil base and does not dry up the material like ammonia-based cleaning products. Leave the mineral spirits on for 5 minutes. Then, wipe the vinyl clean. For the base bottom and footrest, use a chrome polish product.

Shampoo Area

Barbershops now offer full shampoo service and hair color services, which require sinks like you would find in a hair salon. Chain operations use the standard wall sink/shampoo chair format or the freestanding sink units described below. Due to the cost of plumbing and hookup, fewer barbershops install sinks at all the stations. Running plumbing lines throughout your shop with the installation and hookup can run tens of thousands of dollars. Before designing your barbershop that way, do your homework on costs. Many barbershops make the sink area an attractive, visible zone utilizing freestanding shampoo units for a dramatic look. This part of the store can become a profit center for the barbershop, illustrating all possible products the client can buy. One example is a head massage at the sink.

Sink Guideline

# of stations	# of sinks
1	1
2-5	2
6-9	3
10-13	4
14-18	5

These guidelines do not include the color department sinks. You should use the same formula for the amount of sinks if you have a color department.

Wall Sinks

Space-planning a shampoo zone for a wall sink usually has one rule of thumb for measurement: each sink takes up 4 feet of space. Therefore, three sinks will take up 12 feet of wall space. You can go a little smaller, but you should be very careful with spacing for wall sinks. Each sink is about 2 feet wide with 2 feet in between; anything less than that and your shampoo persons and barbers will find it difficult to get in between the shampoo sinks without bumping into the next sink over.

Freestanding Backwash Shampoo Sinks

When space-planning for freestanding backwash sink units, the size is approximately 2 feet wide by 4 feet long, without a footrest. These units are usually spaced on center 30 inches apart from the center of each drain. Doing so gives 6-inches of space in between sinks. There are many ways to design how these sinks are situated, but you always need at least 30 inches of clearance behind them for the shampoo person to wash the client's hair.

> **NOTE**
>
> When purchasing freestanding units, be aware of the type of fittings that are supplied for hookup. Many of the fixtures are metric and do not fit easily to American pipe fittings. You will have to get adapters and it will be a time-consuming and aggravating project.

You also must consider a cabinet behind the sinks for shampoos, conditioners, and towels. The rule of thumb is that a freestanding unit is to be at least 54" from the wall to give room for the shampoo person and a cabinet. You can also design the shampoo units to have a gap in between so you can shampoo from the side as well. The plumbing needs to be 48 inches on center.

For the freestanding sinks, usually the floor needs to be cut (expensive) for waste and waterline installation.

For wall-hung sinks, the waste and waterlines can be installed in the wall and cutting the floor is unnecessary. Each location is different and we recommend you review this with your architect for the most cost-effective approach.

If you have a location with a basement, then cutting the floor is not an issue and it is very easy to move pipes and put the sinks where you desire. You will have to insulate the hot water lines in the basement because they are usually exposed. They lose hot water temperature fast, especially in the winter.

Please refer to the diagrams below for the different design layouts:

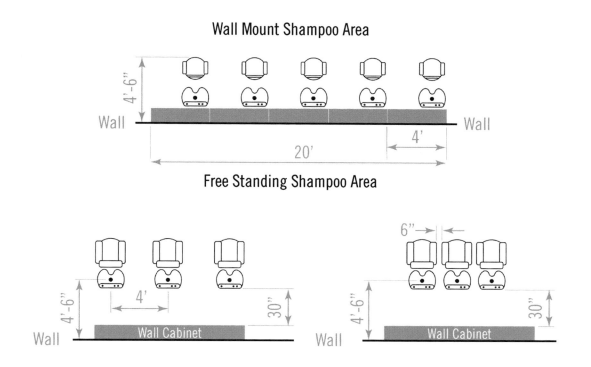

So, as you can see from the illustrations, there are three different ways to design your shampoo area. Be sure you are comfortable with the design you pick.

Pedicure Unit

(This does not apply to many barbershops, but is good information for anyone who is offering pedicure services for men in the barbershop.)

Now, it's time to talk about the pedicure zone. Can you believe over 40 companies manufacture all the different types of pedicure units? It can be very confusing. So, we will break down each style unit for you to decide.

Option 1: Chair with a Separate Footbath

It is the most basic style and the footbath ranges from $30 to $100, depending on the functions. The water must be filled and emptied by the pedicurist for each service. No plumbing is required and the "plastic" footbath needs to be sanitized after each use.

Option 2: Chair with a Separate Footbath that Has a Built-in Pump

This unit is portable and can be put into a closet and taken out for a single use. After use, the unit needs to be brought (on wheels) over to a sink or toilet to discharge the dirty water, which is done by the pump in the unit. The price range for this type of unit is $775–$1100.

Option 3: Pedicure Unit Built Like a "Shoeshine" Bench

These do look very good and have a nice, cozy appeal. They can be built three different ways:

a. Least expensive: unit with a portable footbath (described in #1)

b. Unit with a built-in, flush-mounted sink (kitchen style) which gives the pedicurist water for filling and draining.

c. Unit with a whirlpool sink which looks like a kitchen sink, but contains the whirlpool capability with pumps built-in underneath the unit.

All of these built-in units look great and can usually be ordered in a color to match the rest of the barbershop. But, they all have the same common problem—the unit has no height adjustments.

The benches are designed to sit at a certain height. Many companies design the bench for an average person 5'6" tall. Let's say you have a male client that is 6'4" tall. When they sit in the unit, their knees are up to their chest! Anyone shorter than 5'6" will need to slide down just to reach the bowl. Usually, pillows need to be propped for that person. Too tall or too short, the pedicure becomes an uncomfortable experience without an adjustment for height.

Some of these units come with nice options. But, the bottom line is if they have no height adjustment, they will not work well for most of your clients. Another possible issue is that these units are made of wood—most of them are plywood. If water splashes on the surface and it's not sealed properly, the wood will swell or the Formica will delaminate over time. The price range for these units start at $800 for the base model and can go up to $4000 for all the bells and whistles.

Option 4: Pedicure Unit with a Piped Whirlpool System

This type unit has been in the industry for a long time. What we mean by "piped" is that tubes are running inside the unit and water gets pushed through the pipes by a motor, then it is blown through jets that create a whirlpool action.

Over the last ten years, states have outlawed this type of unit. The reason is that after you use the unit, a small amount of water is left in the tubes inside of the unit. There is no way to sanitize the unit completely by flushing the system. If the unit is not used, the small amount of water left in the pipes builds bacteria, a natural process. Once the unit gets used again, bacteria may affect the client and create a rash or open sores. There are documented cases of this and we do not recommend this style unit. If you do buy this system, carry good insurance!! The unit ranges from $1300–$2000.

Option 5: Pedicure Unit with a "Pipeless" Whirlpool System.

A "pipeless" pedicure unit has all the same functions as the "piped" unit except it has no pipe. It contains a motor that is built behind a fan and it is mounted inside the tub that is covered by a plate. The plate protects you from any injury. The motor turns the fan which creates a whirlpool. After use, you take the cover off and sanitize it so there is no issue of bacteria. There are many types of units and the price range begins at $1800 and goes up to $12,000. My recommendation is that you buy this item from an established dealer. With a lot of these units, you have problems, regardless of brand, quality, or cost. You want to choose a reputable company so that you can count on them to still be in business when a problem arises with the unit.

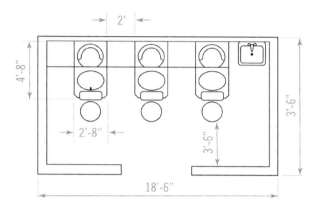

Manicure Area

(Again, this does not apply to many barbershops, but is good information for anyone who is offering manicure services for men in their barbershop.)

Now that we have finished the pedicure zone, we should talk about the manicure or nail department. What we have found, in our experience, is that most commissioned nail technicians/manicurists make on average about 70 percent commission. Once you buy supplies and handle all of the appointments, you are lucky to make 10 percent. Barbershops have manicurists as a service for their clients to offer a full menu of grooming services and create more loyalty.

Our suggestion is that you rent the nail zone out and let your nail technicians buy their own supplies. If you compare the numbers, you will make more money renting this department out with fewer headaches. Following is a diagram to space-plan the zone. Keeping the following dimensions in mind:

- The normal size of a table is 48 inches long by 18 inches wide.
- The height of the table should be 30 inches.

We suggest that manicure tables be positioned against a wall and spaced 6 feet apart. That gives enough room for the client and nail technician to be comfortable.

Below is typical spacing for manicure tables.

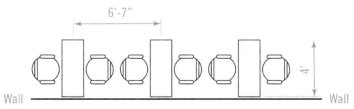

Color Department

The color department is an area where you can make money! This can be the most profitable department. There is no reason why you can't profit by offering color services at your barbershop. It can be designed several different ways.

However, for a barbershop, many men like privacy for hair color services. So, we recommend a dedicated area or room to work in. Provide a television and magazines inside your hair color room so that your male clients don't have to go out onto the main floor of your barbershop for entertainment or to find themselves something to read. Privacy creates a more comfortable, exclusive environment, especially for the male client.

Dispensary

For color services, a dispensary is necessary. The latest trend in hair salons is to have a dining-room style table with hydraulic styling chairs based around it and the colorist just brings a trolley over to work on the client. All the color mixing is done at a "color bar" (shown below) rather than in a dispensary. This could work in a barbershop setting if you set up the color bar in a separate room for hair color services. Styles of color labs:

- Stainless steel
- Upper cabinet built with slots for color tube separation
- Sink for water capability
- Storage for all bowls and brushes
- Sizes range from 4–12 feet in length

Alternatively, you might have a typical dispensary area that also houses your utility appliances and provides a break area for your employees, a necessary part of your barbershop. The diagram that follows illustrates a typical dispensary area. We have found that a dispensary measuring 13' x 14' (as shown) is suitable for most barbershops. Within this space, plan for a washer, dryer, hot water heater, sink, refrigerator, and an eating area. You may want to consider adding lockers for staff so they have a place to store personal items. You can purchase preassembled lockers from Sandusky Cabinets online at www.sanduskycabinets.com.

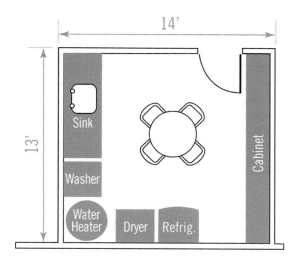

Each barbershop design is different and some cannot support such a spacious zone as the one above.

Hair Dryers

Most barbershops should only start with one dryer, unless they have a strong color business.

You can either hang a dryer from a wall, buy a complete dryer and chair (floor space size 24W x 48L) and place it where you want or get a portable dryer on wheels and be able to store it away when not being used.

The size of a typical dryer chair is 24 wide by 36 inches long. The weight is approximately 60 pounds including the dryer. When space-planning, please make sure that you have ample electric for power. Each dryer draws 9.8 amps at maximum use; we recommend you have access to a 20 amp plug.

Facial/Massage Area

The last department to talk about is the facial/massage area you might put into your barbershop. Following is a typical design for a three-room layout. Two of the rooms are for facials and the other is for massage. A shower can be added, but considering the cost involved, it is like adding another bathroom.

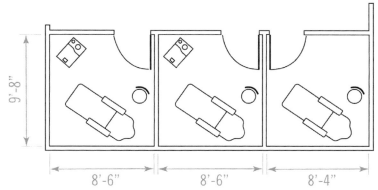

THE GOOD, THE BAD & THE UGLY

(Brought to you by barbershop and salon owners and other industry leaders)

The Ultimate Barber Lounge, Tone McGill, Charlotte, NC

"When designing my barbershop, I reached out to the ones closest to me for help, like my wife, sisters, mother, and father. They really were a big help with the entire process from start to finish."

Kayte G., House of Style

"My first salon I designed myself. I had no experience and wanted to do things my way. The mistakes I made cost me in the long run. I had stylists who wanted to join my team, but I did not have enough space. If I would have laid it out better, I would have had the room for growth. Use a salon professional or architect who has designed salons. It may cost you a few dollars, but you will be better off with the outcome! Once you design it, you are stuck with it for a long time. Make sure you are happy and it works for you and your team."

CHAPTER 15

Observing Different Styles of Barber Chairs

When looking at a barber chair, there are subtle differences of which you should be aware of. These differences can make your clients' experience with your barbershop either enjoyable or disastrous. So, here are some things to look for when purchasing your chair. Let's begin with a little background on barber chairs. Barbering has been around since the beginning of time and I am sure the Greeks and Romans had some type of "specialty" chair they used. For our purposes, we are going to begin with barber chairs of the modern era.

American Barber Chairs

Let's start with the American barber chair. At the start of the 20th century, there were three companies that stood out and helped shape and distinguish what the "classic" barber chair has developed into today. The three companies are Theo A. Koch, Emil Paidar, and Koken Manufacturing. All of these companies made strong, heavy, durable chairs using a combination of steel, porcelain, and fine leather. Some of the options were for the chair to lean back for shaving and shampooing. When the chair back was pushed down, the leg rest would lift up and pivot at the same time, creating a comfortable reclining position for the client. The chairs were designed to weigh between 150–200 pounds, so even in this reclining position the chair would not tip over. All of them had adjustable headrests for comfort and the leg rest was cushioned for the leg to rest upon.

One thing that is missing from barber chairs today is the ash tray. This was a standard feature on most chairs up until the 1980s, when smoking was allowed in any commercial establishment. Now, ash trays are nonexistent. Another feature that has almost disappeared is the "smock" or "apron" holder. This was a bar that was attached somewhere on the chair to hold the client's smock so it was easy to grab when someone sat in the chair. The quality of these chairs was excellent and you can still find some working in barbershops today.

Some antique barber chairs can be found on Craigslist or eBay, as well as equipment distributors based around the country. Antique barber chairs can be purchased from $50 to $5000 or even more. How badly do you want the chair and is the seller really interested in letting it go? Some things to also consider if you decide to purchase an older (antique) chair: Can you get parts for it if it breaks? Who knows how to fix it? If you have a sink, will it fit underneath? Do you need to recover the chair? What's the condition of the hydraulic pump? When buying used equipment, you can hit a jackpot or buy a lemon, those are the risks you take. You have to decide if the risks are worth taking.

Here are some things to consider. Most used barber chairs need to be reupholstered when you get them. It's important that you realize the cost to recover the chair will be in the range of $300 to $500. Not only the recovery, but as you take apart the chair, you may want to replace or "re-chrome" some of the chrome parts. This will be very costly, somewhere in the range of $500–$1000, it all depends on how much work you need to do. This does not include any work you may need to do on the hydraulic pump. If you need a new part, you will have to have it made at a machine shop, because replacement parts are impossible to find. The barber chair may have some wood on it that will have to be sanded down and varnished, which is time consuming and costly. So, if you want to buy an antique barber chair, be prepared for some extra expenses. As long as you are prepared and have a passion for it, you will love it!!

European Barber Chairs

Next, we'll look at European barber chairs. In Europe, most barbers use a regular styling chair for men. Manufacturers began making larger versions of their chairs when international demand began to call for an "authentic" barber chair. So they made the same styling chair larger with a slightly larger base, but without the feel of a "big, bulky men's chair." The European chair was always beautifully designed, but did not function well in the American barber market. The chairs did not come with a footrest. Industry professionals asked to have a footrest; however, when the newly designed chairs with footrests came out, they were either an inch too long or too short. Footrests were also not designed to handle the weight of the client and would loosen over time. Some of the other issues were the back of the chair not reclining far enough back to reach a sink to shampoo a client. Also, the weight of the chair was light and would tip when someone got off the chair and put weight on the footrest. In the present European market, there are now chairs manufactured for the "men's grooming" market. In most cases, these are being made because of international demand.

European chairs do not have the typical "classic barber chair" look. Instead, they have produced a stylish, more modern looking chair.

But, be careful with these types of chairs. Unless the chair is at the lowest position, the chair may tip if someone "stands" on the footrest as they are getting up or sitting down into the chair. Also, this style chair may not fit underneath your sink. So, be sure to check all measurements and whether it will work for you and your barbershop.

Far East Barber Chairs

Now we can address chairs in the Far East. Japan has always been the leader of high quality, high tech barber chairs. One company in particular, Takara Belmont, makes barber chairs that can cost up to $10,000 each. These chairs have all the electronic bells and whistles for your client. One thing to consider when purchasing this chair is the electronics. What if it breaks down? How quickly can you get it fixed? Takara Belmont has a service department, so don't worry if you do purchase this type of chair from them. Other companies sell or manufacture electronic chairs. Before you purchase chairs from them, check the history of the chair as well as the company you are buying it from.

Another area in the Far East is China, the biggest exporting company in the world. They have been active in the beauty industry internationally since the late 1970s. We began working with a few companies based in China in the mid-1980s and the barber chairs that they were manufacturing at the time were, on average, too small for the American market. Several parts of the chair needed to be changed. The seat needed to be wider, the base needed to be wider as well, and the back was too long and clients could not get their head in a shampoo bowl. One thing the Chinese manufacturers did was to listen to their buyer and make changes to the furniture so it fit the American market better. They reacted quickly, made the modifications, and for the last 10–15 years have dominated the American market in volume.

Chinese Manufacturers have done a great job of introducing a lower priced barber chair to the American market. There are some things to take into consideration. Many of the chairs are not made with the quality of the barber chairs of yesteryear that we are accustomed to. Remember the old adage, "You get what you pay for." Presently, the furniture coming out of China has improved dramatically and there are a few manufacturers that make a good quality product for the money. Just remember to buy it from a company that backs up the chair with a warranty.

Here are some pointers to look for as you select the chairs for your barbershop:

- If you are remodeling your shop and you have a sink at each station, make sure the chair goes low enough to get underneath the sink.
- Check the width of the chair and make sure it is wide enough to be comfortable and accommodate your larger clients who will need wider chairs.
- Look at the weight of the chair for tipping.
- Check the bottom base plate and see if it is wide enough so the chair does not tip.
- Inspect the footrest, see how it is made, and look for how it is mounted.
- Check the quality of the product, look closely at the screws and bolts, and see if the chairs are in complete alignment. What that means is to check the smoothness of the hydraulic pump, see how the tilt-back mechanism moves, and look at how it goes back and pulls back up.
- Check the headrest and how it is engineered and works.

The most important point is to buy your chair, new or used, from a reputable dealer. See how long they have been in business, check some referrals, ask who recently bought that chair and see if you can call them and get their opinion of the chair. Remember, this is a large investment—thousands of dollars—so you want to make the right decision and don't want to be stuck with a barber chair that is not practical and falls apart after six months.

After buying your barber chair, make sure you have the delivery handled by a professional. If it is coming from a commercial freight company, I recommend getting one of their trucks with a lift gate. Usually, they just drop the merchandise off at the street and you need to take it off the truck and bring it inside. It would be worth paying a premium to have them bring it in for you. The chair and crate combined can easily weigh over 200 pounds.

SPACE PLANNING – REMINDER

Barber chairs take up more space than a regular styling chair, so when you are designing your barbershop, remember you need at least 5' 0" per station, at a minimum.

Chair Maintenance Tips for You and Your Barbers

○ To clean the **vinyl** on your barber chair, use mineral spirits. Dampen a cloth with the solution and wipe the vinyl down, allowing the product to loosen up all the dirt collected on the vinyl. The reason for using mineral spirits is because it has an oil base and will not hurt the material.

○ To clean **real leather**, use leather cleaner like Armor All®.

○ If the hydraulic pump starts forming an oil ring around the baseline, then that means the pump is leaking and the seals need to be replaced. If it is a newer pump, the unit may be sealed and cannot be fixed. Call the company you got it from and see if they can just replace the pump cylinder, which will save you some money.

CHAPTER 16

What a Barber Demands & Expects
from a Barber Chair

"A barber's chair is only a seat covered with leather. It's not the chair that makes the barber; it's the barber who makes the chair."

—Jeff Grissler (Author)

The American barber has proven a demanding customer to the salon equipment industry since the earliest days of our nation. The efficiency, accessibility, and comfort of the barber chair remains an ongoing priority to the barber, who relies on their client's returning business. Many of today's most basic features of a barber chair were previously unrealized until the 1875 advent of the reclining and revolving barber chair. While this design still serves as the basis for the modern barber chair, technological and social changes have left their mark.

The barber chair is one of the most durable chairs made. Most barber chairs today are made with a footrest and headrest in which a patron can get a haircut or shave in comfort and ease. A person large or small should be able to relax in one of these chairs, so much so, that they can easily forget they're not at home sitting in their reclining chair, but at their favorite barbershop. Gone are the ash trays that use to be a standard in almost every barber chair made. It was okay years ago to have a cigarette or cigar while getting your haircut or a shave.

The barber chair is meant to turn heads with its clean lines and shiny chrome base. The barber expects the classic look and so does his customer. The look should be main street barber. But, the barber is most concerned about the comfort of the chair and knowing that his customer is comfortable and relaxed from his busy day. This chair should entice the customer to swap stories with friends and take a break from life's everyday stresses.

Most barbers do not realize what goes into the design, construction, and manufacture process for these specific chairs. The construction process of building a barber chair requires a lot of time and skill. Barber chairs are generally made with leather and medal. Some are still being made with pure mahogany wood. They are made in factories here in the U.S. and abroad by skilled artisans who know their craft very well. In some cases, the work is still being done by hand.

Barber chairs have to be made with extra care and strength due to the constant use and the ability to recline almost in a full vertical position. Barbers expect their chairs to last long into their careers. In the past, it was not uncommon for a good barber's chair to outlast the life of the barber who used it. Some barbershops have literally used the same chairs with new upholstery for years—even decades—which testifies to their longevity, since barber chairs are rarely replaced. The barbers today expect the same type of quality as barber chairs from the past.

Today's barber chairs are made with extreme qualities and distinctions—some are the traditional style with clean lines and shiny chrome. Featuring fine-crafted leather, newer barber chairs are modeled after the leather interiors of a Porsche or Jaguar. For the non-traditionalist, there are modern era chairs with no sharp edges and no visible screws. They work wonderfully in the barbershop, but can also blend into most salon atmospheres as well.

As we mentioned in the onset of this chapter, these chairs are durable and are made to last. Let us break down each part to explain in detail what you are, the barber, should expect in your barber chair.

- **Materials:** Advances in manufacturing and cost reducing processes have paved the way to a primarily steel, wood, and vinyl built barber chair. This combination of materials gives lasting strength while reducing the overall cost of the chair. Specifically, replacement of leather in specific styles to vinyl has increased the durability of the chair due to its moisture resistance, a concern for many barbers who work at combination wet/dry stations.

- **Hydraulics:** Barbers require the most robust hydraulics in the industry. A typical barber chair should weigh well over a hundred pounds. Add a customer, and it becomes clear why a 400lb+ rated hydraulic should be considered industry standard. In addition to the lift capacity, travel distance is the second most import feature of a hydraulic. A hydraulic unable to meet the height requirements of a tall barber will serve as an annoyance at the least and all day discomfort at the worst. Standard travel range measuring from the bottom of the chair will be approximately 22–30 inches on a manual hydraulic and 16–27 inches with electric bases.

- **Recline:** Many features can be found when it comes to the reclining capabilities of a barber chair. Removable headrests allow easy access to a wet/dry station and should detach with a simple release button on the rear of the chair. Higher-end chairs often feature extending footrests as an added feature to the general leg extension and offer taller clients more comfortable recline positions. Barbers should look for chairs with dual recline releases on each side of the chair, and if possible test the chair prior to purchase. These release mechanisms will need to last the lifetime of the chair and should feel strong and sturdy—any problems will most likely place the chair in decommission until it can be repaired.

- **Experience:** Barbering has been through many phases and changes—from the tools available to both the profession and the public, to the experiences designed for and expected by the client. While the traditional small storefront with the barber pole is still the standard, many new barbershops are positioning themselves as men's grooming centers. This new twist on barbering combines traditional services such as hot towel wraps and straight edge razor shaves, with add-ons ranging from manicures and pedicures to facials, massages, and waxing. Build-out of these spaces typically feature high end barber chairs, wood stations with a matching decor, and perks ranging from flat screen televisions to pool tables and bar services.

✓ CHECK
IT OUT

Things to look for when buying your barber chairs:

○ The barber chair seat should be no less than 22 inches wide. You measure that from inside arm to inside arm.

○ The barber chair should pump up to 28 inches in height; no less than that.

○ The barber chair should be able to recline far enough to position the client's head in a sink or bowl, which is normally 31 inches off the floor.

○ Footrest should elevate itself when the chair back reclines.

○ Footrest should be low enough to the floor that the customer should be able to use it as a step to enter or exit the chair.

○ Round base should be no less than 26 inches in diameter; anything less and the chair may tip over.

"THAT'S WHAT THEY SAY"

"In the early 1800s barber chairs were made from elaborately carved wood and plush upholstery, then replaced by cast iron and porcelain in the early 1900s."

THE GOOD, THE BAD & THE UGLY

(Brought to you by barbershop and salon owners and other industry leaders)

John Macantire, Dallas Barbershop

"I bought four used chairs on Craigslist. They are over 60 years old. They came from a barbershop that had been opened back in the early 50's. I had to have the pumps fixed and the chairs reupholstered. They look better and work as if they are brand new. Everyone that comes in my shop loves them. I am so proud to have the history of barbering by having these antique chairs in my shop. They give the true feel and look that I wanted when I dreamed of opening my barbershop years ago."

Ivan Zoot, Andis Company, Director of Education and Customer Engagement

Q: What does a barber expect in his barber chair?

A: "Cash paying customers! But, if you mean chair characteristics... barber chairs need to rise higher than cosmetology chairs for proper visual reference of necklines, etc. They should spin... and lock in place."

CHAPTER 17

Pricing Your Barbershop Furniture & Equipment

"A price is not the final price until an exchange of money is handed over; so, keep working the deal until that takes place!"

—Eric Ryant (Author)

How to Choose the Right Furniture for Your Barbershop

It's time to place the order for your new barbershop or for your barbershop remodeling project. Are you ready? Or are you dealing with one of these common problems:

- You purchased a chair online. When you received it, you find out that it doesn't fit under the sink.
- The barber chairs that you bought won't angle far enough to reach the sink.
- The chairs you bought for your reception area are too big and the fabric looks more feminine than masculine.

When shopping for barbershop furniture and equipment, there are many things to consider. Selecting the appropriate furniture can add to your barbershop's business and growth. The kind of furniture and equipment you choose determines the environment of your business. The style and look you choose will determine what types of clients your barbershop will draw. Quality furniture and equipment, placed in an inviting atmosphere, is the perfect complement to a great barbershop environment.

Design Inspiration

Have you ever designed a space that was just for men? If so, you probably started with some inspiration—maybe yours came from something you saw in a magazine or something centered around sports, hunting, fishing, or the outdoors. Whatever it was, it inspired you and helped you to make decisions and choices. Designing your own barbershop and choosing your furniture and equipment is exactly the same type of experience. If you are having trouble nailing down your overall design concept, you might want to call on a friend or an interior designer who can help draw out what you'd like to create and keep your design selections and choices on track. You'll be amazed–and possibly overwhelmed–by all the choices. So, you need to have a firm grasp on your brand, the clients that you want to attract, and the experience that you are trying to create.

Working with a Designer

When choosing furniture you should consider working with a designer who specializes in barbershop layouts. You may want to have someone with you who shares your vision and can give you feedback. This will be helpful as the designer presents different option that meet your budget and design vision. A suitable designer should be able to make the design and purchasing experience simple and easy.

You'll have to decide on styles, sizes, colors, laminates, wood, metal, stained, painted, or natural finishes. Seating can be leather, vinyl, a beautiful fabric, and more. Once again, your designer should be able to guide you through making the right decision and help you choose a style and design that you want for your business. Keep in mind that the fabrics and colors you choose must be durable. Water, hair color, and high volumes of clients in a day can be hard on furniture. So, quality should be a factor in your decision.

The furniture and equipment manufacturers and/or distributors will be able to furnish you with catalogs, swatches, and color samples of their products. They will also walk you through the different sizes and shapes of the furniture and equipment. They will be able to discuss competitive pricing, customer service, warranty, and repair policies.

Online Purchases

The popularity of the Internet has made it very easy for the barbershop owner to make purchases online with the click of a button. The Internet is your "friend" when seeking affordable furniture and equipment. It also gives you the ability to build a budget based on a couple of different looks that you might want to create.

If budget is a concern, the Internet may be the best bet for both your furniture and equipment purchases. There are pros and cons when shopping for barbershop furniture and equipment online. It's easy to return a shirt when you buy it online. If the color, fit, or quality isn't what you expected, you can stick it in a box and send it back through the mail. It is difficult to send back a barber chair, workstation, or shampoo sink/bowl. If you don't like it or you feel the quality will not hold up in your barbershop, then you are looking at expensive return shipment fees. Make sure you check the warranty and return policy before you buy from any company, including those that you find online.

When ordering your barbershop furniture and equipment, did you remember to:

○ Choose a durable laminate for your workstations, dispensary, and shampoo areas?

○ Choose a barber chair that fits under your bowl and has the right angle or pitch?

○ Choose a desk that can service all your needs?

○ Create a retail area with the male client in mind?

○ Read all state and city codes for the amount of sinks and stations related to barbershops before ordering the quantities?

○ Choose a shampoo backwash unit that has a lot of adjustments for client comfort?

○ Design a wet- and dry-towel storage area to meet state board standards?

○ Allow adequate space for your barber chair to turn and make sure you have enough space at your location before ordering that special chair?

○ Explore other furniture and equipment for different services if the space has some options? (e.g., color lab/dispensary, pedicure, manicure, facials, massage, etc.)

○ Look at what you need in your office and backroom?

○ Consider "entertainment" for the client who is waiting? (e.g., pool and foosball tables, gaming/laptop areas, coffee bar, liquor/beer bar, etc.)

Furniture & Equipment Budget/Pricing

We have put together different furniture and equipment budgets based on three different types of barbershops: budget, mid-range, and high-end. This should give you the formula you need to pick the furniture and equipment that best suits your budget and style.

Budget Style Barbershop—Furniture & Equipment Pricing Breakdown (Example)

The table below contains pricing that is possible. However, products at this price point may not hold up or withstand the constant use you can expect at a busy barbershop. Although you may able to find these products through various outlets, we suggest that you purchase at the next pricing structure.

	Per Unit	4-Station	6-Station	8-Station
Barber chairs	$400.00	$1,600.00	$2,400.00	$3,200.00
Barber stations	$150.00	$600.00	$900.00	$1,200.00
Mirrors	$75.00	$300.00	$450.00	$600.00
Sink	$175.00	$350.00	$525.00	$700.00
Shampoo chair	$125.00	$250.00	$375.00	$500.00
Dry sterilizer	$150.00	$600.00	$900.00	$1,200.00
Shampoo cabinet	$300.00	$600.00	$900.00	$1,200.00
Hot towel cabinet	$250.00	$500.00	$500.00	$1,000.00
Reception desk	$400.00+	$400.00	$400.00	$600.00
Retail unit	$250.00	$250.00	$250.00	$500.00
Reception chairs	$80.00	$320.00	$320.00	$480.00
Shipping		$1,500.00	$2,200.00	$3,000.00
	TOTALS	**$7,270.00**	**$10,120.00**	**$14,180.00**
Dryer chairs	$350.00	$350.00	$350.00	$350.00
Facial steamer	$180.00	$180.00	$180.00	$180.00
Nail/manicure table (*one per barber shop*)	$140.00	$140.00	$140.00	$140.00
Pedicure unit	$600.00	$600.00	$600.00	$600.00
Color trolley (*one per barber shop*)	$125.00	$125.00	$125.00	$125.00
Stool (*one per barber shop*)	$75.00	$75.00	$75.00	$75.00

NOTES:

SINKS: One sink for every station or 3 sinks for an 8-station barbershop is traditional.

RECEPTION DESK: For the 8-station shop, a larger desk is needed.

RETAIL: For an 8-station shop, a second retail unit is recommended.

RECEPTION CHAIRS: For 4- and 6-stations, 4 chairs are recommended and 6 chairs for 8-stations.

DRYERS: These are optional, all depending on the services you offer.

NAIL/MANICURE TABLE: This is optional, depending on the services you offer.

PEDICURE UNIT: This is optional, depending on the services you offer.

COLOR TROLLEY: This is optional, depending on the services you offer.

STOOLS: These are optional for barbers/colorists/manicurist/pedicurists.

Other items, such as a shoeshine bench, deluxe shaving services, massage/facial furniture/equipment, pool tables, foosball tables, etc. can also be included. However, most of the budget-style shops do not have these services or amenities.

Mid-Range Style Barbershop–Furniture & Equipment Pricing Breakdown (Example)

	Per Unit	4-Station	6-Station	8-Station
Barber chairs	$700.00	$2,800.00	$4,200.00	$5,600.00
Barber stations	$500.00	$2,000.00	$3,000.00	$4,000.00
Mirrors	$150.00	$600.00	$900.00	$1,200.00
Sink & shampoo chair combined	$700.00	$1,400.00	$1,400.00	$2,100.00
Dry sterilizer	$150.00	$600.00	$900.00	$1,200.00
Shampoo cabinet	$600.00	$1,200.00	$1,200.00	$1,800.00
Hot towel cabinet	$300.00	$600.00	$900.00	$1,200.00
Reception desk	$1,000.00+	$1,000.00	$1,500.00	$2,000.00
Retail unit	$900.00	$900.00	$900.00	$1,800.00
Reception chairs	$200.00	$800.00	$800.00	$1,200.00
Shipping		$2,000.00	$2,600.00	$3,500.00
	TOTALS	**$13,900.00**	**$18,300.00**	**$25,600.00**
Dryer chairs	$600.00	$600.00	$600.00	$600.00
Facial steamer	$180.00	$180.00	$180.00	$180.00
Nail/manicure table	$400.00	$400.00	$800.00	$800.00
Pedicure unit	$2,500.00	$2,500.00	$2,500.00	$5,000.00
Color trolley	$150.00	$150.00	$300.00	$300.00
Stool	$150.00	$150.00	$300.00	$300.00

NOTES:

SINKS: One sink for every station or 3 sinks for an 8-station barbershop is traditional.

RECEPTION DESK: For the 6- and 8-station shop, a larger desk is needed.

RETAIL: For an 8-station shop, a second retail unit is recommended.

RECEPTION CHAIRS: For 4- and 6-stations, 4 chairs are recommended and 6 chairs for 8-stations.

DRYERS: These are optional, all depending on the services you offer.

NAIL/MANICURE TABLE: This is optional, depending on the services you offer.

PEDICURE UNIT: This is optional, depending on the services you offer.

COLOR TROLLEY: This is optional, depending on the services you offer.

STOOLS: These are optional for barbers/colorists/manicurist/pedicurists.

Other items, such as a shoeshine bench, deluxe shaving services, massage/facial furniture/equipment, pool tables, foosball tables, etc. can also be included.

High-End Barbershop Furniture

The next breakdown we are illustrating is for a high-end barbershop. We have added color stations and processors. We added other services that might be used. You can make your own spreadsheet and determine your own breakdown.

	Per Unit	4-Station	6-Station	8-Station
Barber chairs	$6,000.00	$24,000.00	$36,000.00	$48,000.00
Barber stations	$2,000.00	$8,000.00	$12,000.00	$16,000.00
Stools	$120.00	$120.00	$120.00	$240.00
Mirrors	$300.00	$1,200.00	$1,800.00	$2,400.00
Sink & shampoo chair combined	$2,500.00	$5,000.00	$7,500.00	$7,500.00
Reception desk	$2,000.00	$2,000.00	$5,000.00	$5,000.00
Retail unit	$1,500.00	$1,500.00	$3,000.00	$3,000.00
Reception chairs	$400.00	$1,600.00	$2,400.00	$3,200.00
Nail/manicure table	$800.00	$800.00	$800.00	$1,600.00
Pedicure unit	$5,000.00	$5,000.00	$5,000.00	$10,000.00
Hot towel cabinet	$300.00	$600.00	$900.00	$1,200.00
Shampoo cabinet	$1,200.00	$2,400.00	$2,400.00	$3,600.00
Color trolley	$400.00	$400.00	$400.00	$800.00
Color chairs (2)	$400.00	$400.00	$400.00	$800.00
Color station (1)	$1,500.00	$1,500.00	$1,500.00	$1,500.000
Dryer chairs	$1,000.00	$1,000.00	$1,000.00	$1,000.00
Dispensary	$2,500.00	$2,500.00	$2,500.00	$2,500.00
Facial steamer	$450.00	$450.00	$450.00	$900.00
Facial table/massage table	$3,500.00	$3,500.00	$3,500.00	$3,500.00
Multifunction unit	$2,500.00	$2,500.00	$2,500.00	$2,500.00
Shoeshine bench	$2,000.00	$2,000.00	$2,000.00	$2,000.00
Shipping		$3,500.00	$4,000.00	$5,000.00
	TOTALS	$70,370.00	$95,570.00	$122,240.00

NOTES:

SINKS: Optional to have a sink at every station or several in one area for the whole barbershop.

RECEPTION DESK: For the 8-station shop, a larger desk is needed.

RETAIL: For an 8-station shop, a second retail unit is recommended.

DRYERS: These are optional, all depending on the services you offer.

NAIL/MANICURE TABLE: A second one is recommended for an 8-station barbershop.

PEDICURE UNIT: A second one is recommended for an 8-station barbershop.

All of these prices can vary. These figures will give you some idea of how much each level of shop will cost. You can use these figures as a starting point.

Installation

Installation can get quite costly. Local installation by the furniture/equipment company you are using can cost $500–$1,000 per day. However, the price can vary. Be ready to negotiate with the contractors you may choose. You may be able to negotiate based on how busy the contractor is and how badly they need the work. Here are some general cost guidelines:

- Local installer per-day charge: Rates will start at $300 and can get as high as $1,000, depending on how many people work on your job and the type of contractor you hire.

- Local installation without truck delivery per day by the furniture/equipment company: $750

- Out of town installation: $1,500 per day

Again, these prices again are an average and may vary depending on the complexity of the job, the area, or location of the work, and whether the installation occurs over a weekend or in the evening.

When setting up delivery of your new barbershop furniture and equipment, did you:

- ○ Have the delivery company set up an inside or curbside delivery? If they aren't delivering inside, you will need help.

- ○ Check to see if your new furniture and equipment will fit through the front door of your barbershop?

- ○ Line up your contractor, electrician, and plumber for the next day after the delivery?

- ○ Schedule help to arrive closer to the time when the equipment will be delivered? Usually equipment deliveries come in the afternoon. No need to have expensive help standing around waiting for a delivery.

- ○ Inform staff to prepare for delivery, help set up, and prepare for opening or grand reopening?

- ○ Inform garbage service that you will need additional removal of boxes and crates?

- ○ Notify clients that you will be closing for a remodel and install of new equipment?

THE GOOD, THE BAD & THE UGLY

(Brought to you by barbershop and salon owners and other industry leaders)

The Ultimate Barber Lounge, Tone McGill, Charlotte, NC

"The only major problem I had was that I decided on candy-apple red barber chairs. They looked great and they were perfect for the overall look that I wanted to achieve. But, they are hard to keep clean and the barbers don't seem to understand how important they are and how expensive they were."

JT, Crazy Style Cutz

"When I opened my first salon, I bought chairs for less than $200. I didn't have a lot of money. The chairs looked good, but didn't last long because of the constant use. I now have better quality chairs and my clients seem happier. Remember, you get what you pay for."

Juliana's New Look Hair Salon

"I bought a lot of my furniture online. It looked good in the pictures, but wasn't exactly what I thought. Price was right, but should have done more homework before buying."

CHAPTER 18

Your Retail Zone

"In designing and baiting a mousetrap with cheese, always remember to leave room for the mouse."

—Saki

Retailing is a business within your barbershop that will make you money. Why is the backbone of most barbershop businesses overlooked and usually thrown together at the end of a new build or remodel project?

The reason: Barbershop owners may not realize that retailing is essential for their business' success and did not give this area the attention it deserved during the space-planning and design process for their barbershop. Most barbershop owners focus on the service side of their business because that's where most of their experience lies. After all, that's why you opened your barbershop, to provide barbering and men's grooming services, right?

It's a common oversight. But, if you started reading this book before starting your project and you picked the right designer, then you would have had the knowledge and the guidance to plan your retail zone right from the beginning.

Make sure that you plan and budget for this space. Your retail department must fit into the concept and design of the barbershop and should not be overlooked when designing and furnishing the space you have chosen for your retail area and displays.

The design and layout process is exhausting and it will take a significant amount of effort and time to plan it properly. Once it is set, you don't want to go back and make last minute changes to "squeeze in" a retail area. And, you definitely don't want to make changes once you hit the expensive construction phase of your project. By planning properly, you will have budgeted for the build-out of this zone. Your investment in this area will make it easier to showcase your retail products. This chapter will help you choose the right fixtures for your selected retail area. Like furnishings in your home, the goal is to make it comfortable and convenient for those who work there and for the people who visit. The furnishings and display areas you choose should make it easy for the clients to browse and buy the retail products you are selling.

The most effective way to choose what type of fixtures and layout you like is by visiting other barbershops in and around your neighborhood. Studying barbershops or other stores that sell products like those used in the men's grooming industry will give you some great ideas for the types of displays that you like and designs that fit your location, style, and clientele. Using other peoples' ideas and modifying them to make them a natural fit for your space is an effective way to come up with exactly what you need to be successful in retail. Make sure you visit on a Saturday when barbershops and retail stores are busier. Then, you can see how the traffic flows in and out of the barbershop and around the retail areas.

Fine-Tune Your Plan

Your retail layout isn't ready until you can visualize it from your clients' perspective. In our experience, the most effective way to lay out a barbershop retail zone is by using empty boxes. The boxes should be placed where you are thinking about putting your display cases or shelving. Doing so will allow you to try all variations of your retail layout. This method should give you a perfect image of how things will look when you are ready to get your actual furniture and equipment. Invite some of your friends and families to fill the space so that you can see how the traffic will flow with your setup. Remember, once fixtures are put into place, they are not easy to move.

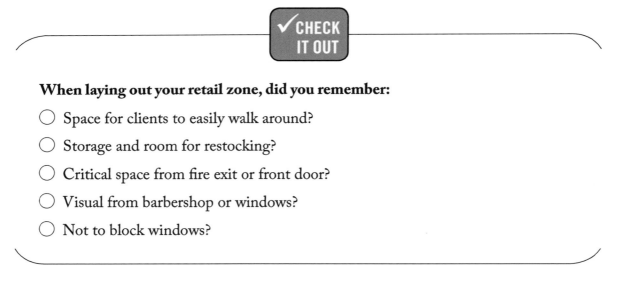

When laying out your retail zone, did you remember:

- ◯ Space for clients to easily walk around?
- ◯ Storage and room for restocking?
- ◯ Critical space from fire exit or front door?
- ◯ Visual from barbershop or windows?
- ◯ Not to block windows?

Selecting Primary Fixtures

We can't emphasize enough the importance of your retail area. Some product suppliers/manufacturers offer branded retail displays that you can purchase and use to display your retail products. For example, L'Oreal has created a brand of retail display cases that emphasize space efficiency and provide a sleek, handsome look to enhance any barbershop.

If your product supplier does not offer a branded option for retail display, then you will need to work with your designer. They can help you sort through the different looks and options for every budget and tailor something just for you.

The primary fixtures that you choose can be mixed and matched and some can be easily moved and placed in different locations. The type you choose should depend on what fits into your barbershop style, brand, and budget. Below, you will find a list of the most common fixtures found in barbershops around the world.

Bookcases

Most bookcases come in a variety of sizes and are very strong. A good quality bookcase will hold up, even with heavy daily use and high traffic in a busy barbershop. They are usually 7 feet tall and are 36 to 48 inches wide. We have seen barbershops stack these if they have the room, which is very effective. Most come with storage underneath. These units are made out of veneer products and come in a variety of colors.

Gondolas

Commonly referred to as islands, gondolas are open-ended display units with shelves on two or four sides. The most common size is 54 inches high, 48 inches wide, and 36 inches deep. We have seen them with built-in storage units, which make it easy for restocking your retail products.

These units are becoming very popular around the country in all types of haircare businesses, including barbershops. They provide a comfortable approach to display and browse products. Keep in mind; you must have the appropriate room for the gondola units.

Pegboards

A long-standing retail display option, pegboards are the easiest and most cost-effective way to display your retail products. Pegboards are boards that are mounted on walls and frames with rows of holes in them to accept display pegs for your shelving.

We have seen these units in barbershops and retail stores around the world. If you are looking for a quick fix for space, this is it. If you are looking for a high-end look, this is not what you should use. Pegboards are efficient and work, but give a low-budget look. However, if done right and within your overall design parameters, they might give the feel of a "home workshop" to your barbershop.

Racks

Racks are wire or wood display cases that stand alone or hang from retail wall paneling called slat walls. Slat walls have also been used throughout the haircare industry since we can remember. Many barbershop owners are replacing their rack display cases with stand-alone gondolas or display cases that match the materials used in the rest of the barbershop. Doing so gives cohesiveness throughout the barbershop and a better fit and feel for the retail department to your clients and staff.

Round Rack

These are circular in design and can vary in size and diameter. Most can be adjusted for the height of the product being displayed. Round racks hold a great amount of product and should be used for promotional items.

Cubes

This type of shelving is a freestanding product display. They come in many different sizes. They are a wonderful way to promote one specific product. You must have a good amount of space to use these effectively.

Tables

For flexibility, a few tables that provide a flat surface for seasonal displays or special offers may be a good idea. Portables are commonly used when you are having a sale or for showcasing samples. The nice thing about this is when you have a promotion you can easily take them away when you are done. They can also travel with you to exhibits and shows that you might attend for bridal shows (market your services to the bride who wants to their husband-to-be and his groomsmen looking sharp on the big day.), Chamber of Commerce events, or barbering school presentations/recruiting days.

> **NOTE**
> Tables are also known as impulse tables. Great for moving sale items!

Bins, Barrels, & Baskets

Another set of fixtures that offer flexibility are bins, barrels, and baskets. They can easily be moved or relocated throughout the barbershop and allow you to keep your retail area looking fresh and new.

Bins, barrels, and baskets are a great way to display samples and/or items you may want to discontinue. However, use these sparingly because cluttering up your retail area is not effective, can look disorganized, and have a negative effect on sales.

THE GOOD, THE BAD & THE UGLY

(Brought to you by barbershop and salon owners and other industry leaders)

David Thompson

"Over the last ten years, people's budgets have changed and so has the economy. I'm searching for new ways to make money with the shop. I'm working on a food lounge and recording studio, also doing graphic design and promotions in-house to make extra money."

Darryl Brandt

"We offer shoeshine and shoe repair services. I partnered with a local shoe repair guy and made it a drop-off service. I take a small cut. That way I'm not hampered by having to worry about doing it myself. Another great service is a licensed massage therapist giving chair massages before or after cuts. Again, partner with a local place so maybe they get an hour booking from the sample chair message."

"THAT'S WHAT THEY SAY"

"The great ladies of Rome always had a hairdresser among their slaves; and the rich nobles had private tonsors, as they were then called.

Barbers were so highly prized that a statue was erected to the memory of the first barber of Rome."

CHAPTER 19

Used Furniture—Getting Creative

"One man's trash is another man's treasure."

Believe it or not, there is a big market for used furniture and equipment. It might just take some research to find the right place or the right person who is remodeling their barbershop. You never know; their "trash" might be your treasure. People who are remodeling want to get rid of what they have. The equipment dealer in the area probably offered them "next to nothing" for their used equipment; so, they decided to sell it on their own. This is a good opportunity to save some money. Here are different ways to locate used furniture and equipment:

- Craigslist (www.craigslist.com): Find your local or regional area on the site.
- Local newspapers: go to the classified section and look under furniture.
- eBay: check out the site, you might find some used furniture available.
- Barbershop furniture supplier: you never know when they might have clearance or slightly used items for sale.

It is important to realize that there are limitations to used equipment. We don't recommend buying any used plumbing products, unless you have the history on the item. All of these items will not have a warranty when bought used and parts may be nonexistent, especially old barber chairs.

Consider used furniture for guest seating, barber chairs, tables, or workstations. However, if you are mixing and matching old and new, then putting the used items throughout your barbershop can save you a lot of money.

> **NOTE**
>
> We recommend that you only buy used equipment from a local source so you can test and look closely at the merchandise before you buy it.

On the following page is a chart comparing the differences in used and new costs for budget-priced versus expensive furniture and equipment. As mentioned in a previous chapter, you might be able to get better pricing from someone who is remodeling and is desperate to sell their old furniture and equipment.

The prices below are slightly higher because, in this case, the seller is putting the product on the market, but is not desperately seeking a buyer. Keep in mind that the prices below do not include any type of shipping or delivery.

Furniture Comparison				
	Budget		Expensive	
	Used	New	Used	New
Barber chairs	$300.00	$600.00	$750.00	$6000.00
Dryer chairs	$150.00	$350.00	$200.00	$1000.00
Sink only	$75.00	$175.00	$150.00	$600.00
Shampoo chair only	$50.00	$125.00	$125.00	$350.00
Reception desk	$300.00	$800.00	$750.00	$2,000.00
Retail unit	$100.00	$250.00	$300.00	$1,500.00
Reception chairs	$25.00	$80.00	$100.00	$400.00
Nail table	$50.00	$140.00	$125.00	$800.00
Styling stations	$50.00	$150.00	$300.00	$2,000.00
Clothes washer	$150.00	$500.00	$500.00	$1,600.00
Clothes dryer	$150.00	$500.00	$500.00	$1,600.00
Pedicure unit	$200.00	$600.00	$500.00	$5,000.00
Stools	$25.00	$75.00	$50.00	$200.00
Facial steamer	$75.00	$180.00	$150.00	$450.00
Hot towel cabinet	$100.00	$250.00	$150.00	$300.00
Facial table	$75.00	$200.00	$300.00	$3,500.00
Multi-function unit	$200.00	$600.00	$300.00	$2,500.00
Sink vanity	$50.00	$200.00	$150.00	$500.00
Shampoo cabinet	$100.00	$300.00	$200.00	$600.00
Sink & chair combined	$150.00	$500.00	$400.00	$2,500.00
Dry sterilizer	$75.00	$150.00	$300.00	$600.00
Color trolley	$25.00	$80.00	$75.00	$400.00

THE GOOD, THE BAD & THE UGLY

(Brought to you by barbershop and salon owners and other industry leaders)

Mannies' Barbershop

"I bought three beautiful old barber chairs on Craigslist from a barber who was in business over 40 years. He was happy I was going to keep his tradition going. I had the leather replaced and buffed out the metal and they look better than brand new. My clients love them and I love the history behind them."

CHAPTER 20

Selecting the Right Contractor & Architect

Congratulations! You have come a long way. The lease process and negotiations are finished. You have worked with a designer to layout your barbershop. Next on the list is selecting the right architect and contractor. If you are in a shopping center, your landlord may be able to direct you to a known architect and contractor.

Finding & Working with an Architect

First, you will need an architect to get you started. This individual will help design and space-plan your location. You can find businesses that specialize in space-planning and design that also sell barbershop furniture. We highly recommend that you find one of these companies and space-plan for your barbershop before you go to the architect. You will save money with the architect if you get your space-plan done elsewhere. The architect, who is not likely to have experience in designing barbershops, won't have to spend time researching how to space-plan a barbershop.

Here are a couple of websites to help you locate an architect:

- www.architectfinder.aia.org
- www.servicemagic.com

The architect will draw up the blueprints for your new space. It is critical for you to spend a lot of time with the architect to make sure he or she puts everything in the right place.

Once you have the architect's plans, you should move quickly to get some prices on the cost for construction. You want to bid your job and get prices from at least three contractors.

You should plan on giving each contractor four to five sets of plans so that they can rapidly get you a final price. Ask your architect to make 15 sets of plans. It sounds like a lot, but this will save you weeks of time. A contractor usually takes a set of plans, leaves them with a plumber, electrician, and an air conditioning company and calls them back in a few days for their price. If you only get five sets of plans, you can only give one to two sets to each contractor, which will make the bidding/pricing process take longer. Your architect will also give you two copies of "certified plans." These plans are the ones that your "chosen contractor" will be submitting to the city. Do not misplace them or mix them up with the other 15 sets.

Finding & Working with the Contractor

You have spent hours with the architect going over plans and discussing so many different ideas and layouts. You are confident that your ideas are finally down on paper and that you have the look you want. Just one question remains, "Who is going to build it?"

Friends, family, and associates can usually recommend a good contractor. If you cannot find someone you feel comfortable with you can try these websites:

- www.angieslist.com
- www.1800contractor.com
- www.needacontractor.com
- www.agc.org

To help with your contractor selection, we have put together the most important questions you should ask your potential contractor before you hire them.

When selecting and working with contractors, be sure to:

○ **Ask what type of projects they have done.** Many contractors have done various projects, but have they ever built out a barbershop? Do they specialize in cabinetry, or are they more of a generalist that does a bit of everything? If they concentrate on remodeling projects and deal with a variety of subcontractors, plumbers, and electricians, they may be a good fit for your project. A contractor that builds custom homes may not be the wise choice for a barbershop build-out or remodel on a tight budget.

○ **Visit some existing or recently completed projects.** Good builders are proud of their projects. Ask to see photographs or visit the contractor's last few projects. Talk with their last few customers; ask how the contractor handled the job and whether they are happy with the outcome of the project.

○ **Get a list of former clients.** Word of mouth is often the best solution when hiring a contractor or builder. If the contractor gives you five people to call, make sure you call all of them and ask what type of relationship they had with the contractor and would they work with the contractor again.

○ **Check that he is licensed and insured!** You should never hire a contractor who is not licensed and insured. This should protect you against any unseen accidents and/ or liabilities that may arise during your remodel or build-out. More importantly, if a contractor bears the expense of carrying the cost of the license and insurance, they are more likely to be a professional company. Also, if you're borrowing money from a bank, they will require that your contractor has the necessary insurance and license. They will not give you the money needed for your construction if your contractor doesn't carry general liability and Workers' Compensation Insurance.

○ **Ask how long he has been in business.** The fact that a builder or contractor has been in business more than five years is a good thing. It is an indication that the builder can run a successful project and satisfy clients.

○ **Find out who will be running your project.** This is very important to know. If you build a relationship with your contractor, you will feel better if he is on the job every day. If he uses subcontractors and he is going to manage from an office or the back of his truck, you can bet you will not be happy. Smaller contractors are more likely to provide a hands-on approach, which is probably the best option for keeping your project on time and on budget.

○ **Confirm payment terms.** Contractors get paid in many different ways. Before the project starts, agree to terms and sign a written contract on how you are expected to pay.

○ **Never pay in advance or in full.** You always want to stay ahead of your contractor. If you owe your contractor, it ensures that they will complete whatever task is on hand. You will have deadlines to meet. Be sure they will be there for inspections or anything else that comes up. I have heard many horror stories about disappearing contractors.

It is important to choose your contractor in a timely fashion for a few reasons:

1. At this stage, you will probably have already signed the lease and the clock is ticking on the "free" rent period that you may have negotiated for the build-out.

2. If the city rejects the plans, you'll have to go back to the architect and resubmit new plans. This will eat into your "free" rent period. One way to get around this is to negotiate with the landlord and not to pay rent until you get your final "Certificate of Occupancy" (CO) from the city. You can also negotiate with the landlord to start your free rent after your CO (refer to CHAPTER 8: How to Negotiate Your Lease).

THE GOOD, THE BAD & THE UGLY

(Brought to you by barbershop and salon owners and other industry leaders)

Greg Martin, Owner American Haircuts

"I choose my contractor very carefully. It's always better to NEVER get involved with contracting family or friends for work at your barbershop. Look for reputation, check references, and check the Better Business Bureau. Ask for on time build out clauses. Make sure they have a legitimate brick and mortar store front and preferably a showroom for finishing products. Always get at least four bids and look for quality in the bids. Compare them and check that what is being offered/provided in the bids are apples to apples with each other. Accurate bids will all be within a few thousand dollars of each other. If you get a dramatically low bid, it's probably not an accurate one or it's a very hungry contractor that is spread too thin. If you are looking in an unfinished center that promises white box delivery, always start with the on-site contractor. You can almost always get a better deal from them because they are already on-site. Still follow the same reference checking and bidding procedure with them."

James Giodano, Mr. Magoo's Barbershop

"Choosing a family member as your contractor may save you a few dollars. But what happens when the work is not getting done on time or the quality of the work is not what you expected? I had to fire my wife's brother. It's been two years and he still doesn't talk to me."

CHAPTER 21

The Construction Phase

Construction can be the biggest expense when building your barbershop. If you have had any kind of construction done, you know that overruns and lack of knowledge on your part can be expensive. To help keep you from unforeseen expenses and issues during the construction phase, we have identified some of the most common things that you'll need to modify in a typical location.

You should realize that all of these upgrades can be negotiated with the landlord and become his expense, not yours. We recommend that you look at the space very closely and ask the landlord or the leasing agent what the store has and what the lease includes.

Air Conditioning

A typical location in a shopping center usually has an air conditioning unit that is inadequate for a barbershop. Below are what the landlord typically gives and what the shop needs:

- Typical space: one ton for every 400 square feet
- Recommended size: one ton for every 180 square feet

If the landlord does not want to increase the capacity of your A/C unit, then there will be a cost of $1,500 to $2,000 per ton of A/C to increase the size. Each location should be checked thoroughly.

Electrical

The standard-size panel in a normal store is usually 125 amps. That amount is too small and a decent size barbershop needs a panel of 250 amps. Upgrading electrical can get very expensive. To increase an electrical panel, you need to run more wires from the main electrical room in the shopping center. If it is 400 feet away from your space, it will be thousands of dollars to bring in more power. Check your location very carefully.

If you are thinking of renting an older building, wiring may need to be replaced and upgraded to meet the present building codes. This alone can easily run thousands of dollars.

Plumbing

Having the right number of bathrooms to meet state requirements is the biggest issue. If you have six or more barbers or more, most states/counties require two bathrooms. It usually costs about $5,000 to put in a bathroom.

> **NOTE**
>
> With the introduction of added services such as shaves, color services, and pedicures, upgraded and larger hot water heaters are necessary in most barbershops and grooming salons. Remember to add this to your startup expense!

You are best off following the requirements of the state of county. Besides, the second bathroom can double as a changing room. If you look at an 8-station barbershop, you can have as many as 25 people in your barbershop at any given time. One bathroom is in adequate for this many people.

Many times, existing bathrooms do not meet the latest handicap accessibility codes. The county may ask you to make it bigger, change the toilet, and put in a sink that works for wheelchairs. You may have to install handicap rails if they are not there already. Your county may also ask you to install a ramp for access to the bathrooms if your shop has any kind of elevation. The latest codes are for the door to be 36 inches wide and to open out with a lever handle only. The inside must have a 44 inch clearance for a wheelchair to completely turn around in the bathroom. The pipes underneath the sink must have heat-resistant covers to protect a handicapped person's legs underneath the sink.

Another common plumbing issue is the size of the hot water heater. Usually it is too small for a barbershop. A barbershop needs a minimum of an 80-gallon, double-element water heater. Anything less will create a hot water shortage in your shop. The cost is around $500 for an electric water heater. If you have the potential of using a natural gas water heater, this will be more efficient.

Also, remember that you will need a washer (and a dryer) for towels. You will want to make sure that your space can accommodate this addition.

Shampoo Area

It is recommended that this be located near the bathroom or dispensary for two reasons. One, if there is an existing floor, this usually needs to be cut up to install your waste water pipes underneath. The water always needs a downward flow toward the drain; water cannot flow upward to drain. This may not be an issue if you have a

Second, your hot water heater is usually located in the dispensary. If your sinks are far away from that, you have the potential of losing hot water and you will be washing your clients with cold water. This problem can be solved by insulating the water lines. Either way, it will cost you more money.

Traditional barbershops usually have a sink at every station. This can be a very expensive part of your construction because of the extent of plumbing work needed. Water and waste lines need to be run long distances and usually the floor slab needs to be cut and replaced to facilitate this project. If you decide to design your location like this, try to negotiate this part of the project with the landlord and make it his expense.

Drywall or Partition Construction

When searching for a facility, it is preferred that all the walls are open to add electrical, telephone, Internet, and alarms inside the walls before you close them up. Of course, this all depends on the location and whether the location is new or existing. When considering your existing bathroom, this may not be up to code on the size, which means you will have to tear down the existing walls and rebuild the bathroom.

If you're in an older building and your walls are made out of plaster and lathe, it can be very expensive to move walls and make any alterations.

Lighting

The most cost-effective type of ceiling lighting is the standard 2x2 or 2x4 acoustical ceiling lights. They may not be the most attractive, but they will save you thousands of dollars in a year. We have seen barbershops use many types of halogen lights. Halogen lights work very well, but this will really increase your budget. The standard ceiling is usually included when you take the store. If it's not new construction, you may need to replace the covers for the typical fluorescent lights. They may be yellow and look unsightly. You may not have enough lighting in the barbering area and have to add more lights, not something many people realize. These can be negotiated with the landlord if you realize the shortage or the yellowing before you sign your lease.

Reference: www.salonlights.com & www.freestylesystems.com

Ceiling

A landlord will usually give you a standard 2x4 acoustical ceiling. Many barbershops have chosen to go with no ceiling. Beware, leaving an open ceiling will greatly increase your electric bill for A/C or heat over the year. Plus, with all of the duct work and lighting, dust begins to build and every six months you will need a crew to come in and clean it. If you don't schedule regular cleanings, the barbershop will begin to look dirty and unsightly. Most barbershop owners choose to paint their ceilings black, to give an open "infinity" feeling, but this shows dirt immediately.

NOTE

Stained concrete is the latest trend. It is very durable, but hard on the feet and back.

Flooring

Wood, ceramic tile, and rubber are suitable floor types. Our experience has been that all the floors can look amazing in your barbershop; it all depends on the budget you want to spend. One thing you should consider, especially in the shampoo area: water will spill on the floor and once it gets wet, it might become slippery and create a liability issue. When choosing your flooring, remember that whatever product you choose, it must be durable, not slippery when wet, and good on the feet and legs for standing extended periods of time.

✓ **CHECK IT OUT**

Construction items that will blow your budget:

○ Moving hidden electrical and plumbing lines when moving walls

○ Replacing the floor

○ Adding more air conditioning

○ Adding a second bathroom which meets handicap accessibility requirements

○ Updating electrical service

○ One time impact fees from the city or county

CHAPTER 22

Computerizing Your Barbershop

Written by John Harms, President/Founder Harms Software (Millennium)

Computerizing your barbershop can be very intimidating. You may run a first come, first served barbershop. If that's the case and if that's how you want to continue operating, then computerizing may not be something that you need to consider at this point. However, you should look at automation as an opportunity to grow your business. Client loyalty systems, automated email marketing, online booking, gift card purchasing, and other great features help make your business special. Differentiating yourself with memberships, VIP rewards, special pricing, and direct access to your clients via things like text messaging specials or appointment openings can help you retain more clients. If your business and clients would be better served by computerizing, then this chapter will help you answer questions like:

- Why computerize at all?
- When should I start worrying about my software and computers?
- What is a typical plan for computerizing a barbershop?
- Which software should I buy?
- What about ongoing training and support?
- Which computers do I need? Do I need a server? If so, how many other computers should I have?
- What kind of additional hardware would I want to consider (i.e., cash drawers)?

Why Computerize?

Computers have been used in some hair salons since 1980; however, the penetration into the beauty and grooming industry didn't really take hold until the turn of the century. Most people simply used cash registers or a computer as a cash register. As software became more powerful and appointment books could be written that looked and functioned like a true appointment book, the industry began to embrace technology more.

The bottom line: a barbershop that is not computerized cannot serve their clients at the same level as a fully computerized shop. Everything is smoother and faster, from the initial call, to booking the appointment or changing an appointment, to ringing up the sale with integrated credit card processing. Try looking up a gift card balance manually. With a computer, it would take about two seconds. Think about looking up a client's hair color formula using the old-style card files. With a computer, it would take two seconds. As a matter of fact, the computer would know WHICH formula to print out with the daily appointment tickets so that the whole process is smooth and easy for your barbershop staff.

For an appointment-based business, having the right software can help your business to flourish and make your life so much easier. When you computerize your business, you can:

- Store client information (name, phone number, mailing address, emails, etc.) for future marketing and promotional opportunities.
- Automatically pre-book the client's next appointment.
- Quickly move an appointment to a different barber or days/times.
- Access instant statistics on percent booked, pre-booked and more.
- Visualize (by color) what type of appointments is booked.
- Automatically confirm appointments.
- Create standing appointments in seconds—not hours!

The top three reasons to automate your barbershop are:

1. Professionalism and ability to serve your clients efficiently.
2. Enhanced ability to grow and market your business.
3. Security and control.

When Should You Start Worrying About Software & Computers?

Many people think they need to wait until the barbershop is almost ready to open before ordering computers and software. You actually want to plan your computerization as early as the initial architectural phase of your build-out. So many times, barbershop owners underestimate the space required on a desk for monitors, receipt printers, credit card swipe machines, keyboards, and mice. Also, you need to plan the appropriate placement of simple things like grommet holes to hide wires on top of the desk. All-in-one computers and wireless hardware can reduce some of the clutter, but knowing which computers will be used is important when purchasing or building the front desk.

Getting a jump start on data entry is also a good idea. You'll be able to use any client data that you have for pre-opening marketing. You also need to enter all of your products and barcodes into the system, prices, employees, existing client records, employee schedules, and commission structures. It's not an overwhelming task, but it's certainly not something you want to wait to do until the week before you open! Also, you will want to have your staff trained on the new system prior to opening. Many times, the data entry is done off-site at another location while the construction phase is underway. Then, once the "dirty" part of the construction is done, the computers, network, and other hardware are brought in to be installed.

Which Software Should I Choose?

Choosing the right software package comes down to asking the right questions of the software company and yourself. Are you looking for a simple cash register system that gives you some basic reports? If yes, you need to rethink what a computer can do for you. It needs to be more than an appointment book and more than a point-of-sale system. The great news is most software is quite affordable compared to 10 years ago. Many software systems offer subscriptions with little or no money down for a monthly fee that includes support and updates. Be sure to check out the options and pricing models available to you.

Keep in mind, however, that over 50 percent of people who purchase software don't pick the right one the first time. They either overlook key features that are missing or find that the software they purchased isn't ready to grow with them. Then, it's back to the drawing board to research and buy another software package and transfer the data or reenter it! Sound painful? It can be! So, take the time to evaluate your needs, research the software, and—more importantly—research the company behind the software prior to purchasing.

To build a successful barbershop business, you'll need to keep tabs on five key performance indicators:

1. New Clients Per Month
2. New Client Retention
3. Repeat Client Retention
4. Frequency of Visit
5. Average Ticket

Your software must have these key performance indicators to give you the forward focus view of how your business is doing. All software tracks how much revenue you are making in services, retail, gift cards, packages, and so forth. Revenue is important, but it's based on what you did yesterday to grow your business.

The "growth indicators" are the metrics of what you can expect in revenue tomorrow. The good thing is you can affect them today, in the moment, and throughout the day by pre-booking clients and doing the right thing to retain the clients you worked so hard to bring in. Follow the growth indicators on a weekly basis and you'll see your business grow organically one client at a time.

What Is a Typical Plan for Computerizing a Barbershop?

Unfortunately, there is not a one-size-fits-all solution when it comes to setting up your barbershop to be fully automated. Many factors can affect the planning, such as: the size of your business, how many stores, the number of network connections, and the number of computer workstations. However, you will take some definite steps and need to meet key milestones to get your technology infrastructure in place.

Phase I: Research

- Utilize the Internet to search for barbershop software or barbershop management software; keep in mind that you might have to broaden your search and use key word search terms like: hair salon and beauty salon in your search for software. You'll find dozens of options available to you. Look for companies that have been around for more than a couple of years and have shown a dedication to the hair, beauty, and grooming industry. Many companies come and go and you don't want to invest in a fly-by-night company.
- Ask around at industry events. What are other people using? Do they like it? Do they feel they get input into the updates? Does the company have annual conferences and attend industry-specific educational events?

Phase II: Demo/Testing

- Download a trial version of the software or request a demo.
- Schedule a live demonstration with a salesperson and gauge their knowledge of the hair, beauty, and grooming industry.
- Ask for the support phone number and try it a few times before you buy. Does someone answer? Do they know what they are talking about? Do they know the industry? Are they friendly and helpful?

Phase III: Software Selection

- After determining the top three software companies that fit your needs, you'll have to evaluate them on price, length of time in business, number of support staff, features/benefits of the software, and overall feeling you get for the company.
- Once you make a selection, it still takes a few phone calls and decisions before you're ready to start installing the software and entering data.

Phase IV: Hardware Needs Assessment

- It's best if you choose a company that is also knowledgeable in hardware, computers, and the other devices you'll need to run a successful barbershop.
- Ask for a needs assessment based on the size of your barbershop, size of your front desk, number of employees, and budget.

Phase V: Hardware Purchase

- Some computers, when special ordered, take a couple of weeks to ship. When they arrive, the software company can usually install the software for you. So, expect up to three to four weeks for computer delivery. It can come faster if the computers are in stock, but that's not always the case, especially during the busy season.

- During this phase, you should contact local computer service technicians to begin forging a relationship for ongoing support, computer setup, etc.

Phase VI: Network Setup

- You need to decide if you want to run wires for a wired network, which results in faster access to your data. However, if you want to run a wireless system, you will have to purchase computers and an operating system that will work best with a wireless system.

Phase VII: Software Installation

- Your software may be preinstalled on the computers you purchased from your provider. However, if you purchased the computers on your own, you'll need to install the software.

- Even if the software you are using is web-based, there is still configuration and installation of drivers for your equipment.

Phase VIII: Data Entry Training

- Before you start entering data, take the time to get proper training or read the manual on how to enter the data properly.

Phase IX: Data Entry or Data Conversion

- Start pulling old invoices, purchase orders, and service menus together so you can enter them into the software you've purchased.

- Divide the work up amongst your staff so that everyone learns. However, make sure they enter the data consistently. It's important to make sure the data goes in properly so that the reports you run make sense.

- If you are doing a data conversion, see the section later in this chapter on handling your data conversion.

Phase X: Advanced Training & Practice

- Now that your data is entered, you want to get advanced training on the appointment book, register, inventory, management, and security.

- Practice! Some software comes with the ability to create an instance of your data so you can train your employees and practice using the system without affecting the actual data.

Phase XI: Testing for "Go Live"

- Prior to going "live" and opening your barbershop for business with the new system, go through some sample ring-ups, bookings, payrolls, etc. so that you can verify the system is functioning and set up properly.

Phase XII: "Go Live!"

- Fire up the computers and start booking appointments and ringing up all of those sales! Remember, partner with a software company that focuses on making the front desk a power position that helps grow the business!

Data Conversion & Set Up

Once your software is installed, it is time to prepare for your training on the software. If you are going to convert data from an existing software application, it is HIGHLY recommended that a preliminary conversion is performed. A preliminary conversion will allow you to perform your training on the software using your real data. The conversion will give you the opportunity to identify any issues with your conversion and what "tasks" you will need to accomplish once your final conversion has been performed.

Ask your software provider if they have a task sheet specific to your conversion on typical items that should be handled either before or after your conversion. It will save you a lot of time and money if your software provider identifies the key issues that need to be addressed.

Also, ask your software provider if they have an implementation department. That department is specifically designed to walk you through the process of implementing your software and getting you live. They will make sure everything is set for you from the installation of the software, to scheduling your conversions, to performing follow-up calls on the day you go live, which will help ensure this process is as painless as possible.

One key thing to note is that not all software companies have full conversions from other software companies. It is possible that you can lose your client history and that you'll need to start from scratch or enter all the data manually.

It's very important to ask what major data WILL be converted and what major data WILL NOT be converted. For example, in some circumstances, the software company may only be able to convert client information and this would result in a one-time only conversion.

Another important fact for you to consider is that the software company may not be able to convert any data directly from your current software. However, you should find out if there are exporting capabilities via reports or any other method. Your new software company may be able to create custom conversions for you if the data exported is in a readable format.

Once the software is installed or your preliminary conversion has been implemented, you are ready to begin your training and determine a "go live" date. Use this date and work backward to come up with a training schedule. Be sure to check if there are any scheduled staff vacations, holidays, or anything else that may hinder your plan. If your software company has an implementation department, they will be more than happy to work on a game plan for you. As long as you and your staff accomplish your "homework" during your training sessions, you will be able to go live as planned.

Training & Support

How your data is entered and set up from the start will shape how your reports are viewed, how your front desk operates, and how your appointment book will be viewed by all. Most software companies only include a basic training package with the purchase of the software. Be sure to ask what training package options are available to you in order to make an informed decision as to what will be best for your business needs.

If your business is brand-new, the basic training package is usually enough for you to get started. There will be many distractions when opening a new business. Just focusing on the basics of the software is more important than trying to learn everything or using every feature. You should schedule more advanced training later on—once your barbershop has been up and running for a few months.

However, if you are operating an established business with refined processes, the basic training package will not be enough for you. You will require additional training time to fully understand how your new software handles your current procedures. In some cases, the new software will not be able to generate the same reports as before or may not have a feature you were accustomed to using. It's very important you receive additional training time to review current procedures and policies, as this will allow you to update your current training guides for each department.

Your training sessions should be broken up into two groups: management and employees. To keep labor costs down, only include people in training when there is reason to have them present. For example, there is no need to include service providers or front desk staff if you are learning how to enter employee commissions into the software. Be sure to ask what will be covered during each training session so you can include only the appropriate personnel.

DO NOT leave one person in charge of learning the software and setting everything up for your business—that approach always fails. If you place a newly-hired manager, friend, or existing long-time employee in charge of setting up the most important aspect of your business, they will become too stressed. They'll leave, start to hate the new software, hate their job, or contaminate other employees to hate the new software. You'll end up having a coup on your hands and a mess to clean up.

That might be an over-exaggeration of what could happen; but, the point is, use caution if you are thinking this is one person's responsibility. Include yourself, as the business owner, in these training sessions to keep the momentum going and the frustration level controlled.

It will also allow you to make sure the employee or employees in charge of handling this new software installation have the necessary time needed to make this a successful installation.

It is highly recommended that you receive an estimate for the cost of having a software trainer to come to your facility and assist with the training/launch of the software. If you have the budget, this approach is 99 percent effective when it comes to making sure your training is a success. All processes are considered and implemented. Your operations and your clientele may only be minimally affected by this conversion. Having a trainer onsite, who knows the software, can help you during the go live process and ensure that your cash drawers balance to the penny from the very first day.

With any technology change or installation, you can expect bumps in the road. But, having a knowledgeable resource at your facility will be priceless and ensure the success of your software implementation.

Ongoing Training

Once the dust has settled and you've started to master the basics of your software application, it's time to revisit the multitude of features that the software offers. These may be advanced features that caught your attention at the time of purchase. They may include client loyalty programs and allowing clients to earn points for purchases or book appointments online.

Ask your software provider what additional training options are offered. In most cases, such packages are available via DVDs, online Webinars, or additional remote training sessions that have been customized to your desired topics of discussion. Even better, most software companies offer an Annual User Group Conference where you can attend a forum for only current users of the same software. They get together and discuss what they have done with the software to make their business a success and what improvements they would like to see in future versions.

If your software company has an online community forum, we highly recommend you be active on the site and read what others are discussing. The ability to discuss how to implement something new or discuss compensation strategies with other business owners in your industry and hear what has worked and what hasn't will be invaluable to you.

Always be aware of what your software company's rollout plan is for releasing software updates and learn how you can find out what has been addressed/enhanced in the update. Most users think that updates are made to apply fixes to issues. But, many times, new features or reporting capabilities are also released at the same time. The new features are usually released to meet current trends and user requirements. A software release often means new metrics or capabilities to improve your front desk operations and improve your bottom line.

Hardware

Let's take a look at some of the hardware you might need to purchase and some of the questions you might have around technology.

Computers

- Do I need a "real" server? No. If you are just looking to have a small network without online booking or an online store, you can use a fileserver or robust workstation to act as your server. Larger network servers are recommended for:
- Five or more computers
- Several open connections for online booking
- Multiple and different types of software running at the same time
- How many workstations should I get? The answer depends upon the amount of staff and space you have. In an average size barbershop, there would be two computers at the front desk for reservations and check out and another computer in the back for a look-up station and to import service notes for the staff.
- Do I need a computer in the backroom? It does depend on the size of your barbershop. For larger barbershops with more staff and more services, it is highly recommended to have a to "look-up station" in the back of your barbershop to eliminate clutter and personnel swarming at the front desk. Your front desk is a client's first impression. It's best to eliminate as much chaos at the front desk as possible. When employees have a source of checking on appointments and monitoring their metrics, it promotes a more relaxed atmosphere and more informed service providers.

Network

- Wired or wireless? Wired networks are ideal in most scenarios. The data transfer rate is higher and it requires less maintenance than a wireless network. However, wireless networks can be used with tools like Microsoft® Terminal Services and ThinSoft® WinConnect®, allowing you to use portable tablet PCs or eliminate the clutter of wired stations.
- Should I get an Internet connection? The Internet is essential to taking advantage of email and social media marketing, remote backups, and for doing automated updates. It is also an essential element to allow remote support by your software company or if your software is web-based.

Peripheral Equipment

- Cash Drawers: You can choose between USB and serial cash drawers. It is suggested that you purchase USB drawers, as most computers don't come with serial ports anymore. Cash drawers add a layer of security to your front desk because they are locked unless the computer opens the drawer. Each time that occurs, the software you choose should track it in an activity log for your review.
- Receipt Printers: Most receipt printers work well with the software. You may want to purchase a receipt printer that has a mechanism to automatically open your cash drawer, which will allow you to purchase a non-intelligent drawer and save money.

- Other equipment: You might consider a credit card swipe that mounts on the side of your monitor; pole displays to show what the client is purchasing (this is a requirement in certain states or counties); paging systems that alert staff when a client checks in; and more. You might be surprised at all the options you have once you computerize.

Third-Party Vendors

Software companies typically align themselves with third-party partners to enhance the company's offerings as well as negotiate rates and costs on the your behalf. These third-party vendors either integrate directly with the software or offer products and services that conform to the standards of growth and development that the software was designed to offer.

It's very important to learn about the people and companies who are affiliated with the software company and come with such great references. Integrity is everything in this business and only the best software company will align themselves with the best third-party partners. Some examples of third-party involvement or integrations can include, but are not limited to, credit card processing, gift cards and online certificates, and even advanced marketing support.

Credit Card Processing

Software and Point-of-Sale (POS) applications should have the capability to process credit and debit cards directly through the system. Although the functionality exists, the barbershop would still need to establish a merchant account with the recommended third-party partner.

What is a merchant account? It is a specific account set up with a financial institution to allow you to accept credit card payments directly from your clients. You need a merchant account if you want to take credit card payments from your clients through your business name and have the money deposited directly into your business checking account.

There are a variety of merchant acquirers. So, ask the right questions to help ensure that you are receiving the best possible rates, care, and customer service.

Check off the questions below as you ask them:

◯ Is there an application fee?

◯ Is there a programming or setup fee?

◯ What are the "other" fees associated with my merchant account?

◯ Are the quoted rates guaranteed? If so, for how long?

◯ Is there a contract? If so, for how long?

◯ Are there any termination or early cancellation fees?

◯ If there is a problem, who do I talk to?

◯ How long do processed payments take to reach my bank account?

◯ Are there any reserve requirements or hold backs? Can I get that in writing?

◯ What are the hours of operation for customer service?

Gift Cards & Online Gift Certificates

Software and Point-of-Sale (POS) applications should have the capability to integrate with a magnetic strip or bar-coded gift card solution. Gift cards represent your company's brand. The recommended third-party partner should offer a turnkey solution from graphic design to production.

You need a partner with the flexibility and the power to execute a distinct, exciting gift card program that engages and excites your guests, enhances your brand, and strengthens your bottom line. Gift cards are a necessity and considered a "must have" when opening a new barbershop. They are a perfect solution for day-to-day traffic (peer-to-peer interaction). However, a solution must also be considered for Internet and online traffic (non-peer-to-peer traffic).

The solution is quite easy: offer your clients the ability to purchase gift certificates online. This capability is a great service for your clients, providing convenience, instant gratification, and solving last-minute, gift-giving problems. You'll sell more gift certificates and save staff time while doing it. A variety of companies provide this service. Asking the right questions will help ensure that you are receiving the best possible rates, care, and customer service.

Check off the questions below as you ask them:

○ Why do I need your gift card services?

○ What will the gift certificates look like?

○ How does it work?

○ How does it affect my front desk staff?

○ Who typically buys instant gift certificates?

○ How are credit cards processed online?

○ How will my clients receive their gift certificates purchased online?

○ Can I run specials or promotions?

○ How are gratuities handled?

○ What percentage or profit-share do you charge on purchases?

Marketing Support

Software and Point-of-Sale (POS) applications should provide a variety of key marketing and tracking techniques that should help you improve the frequency of visits from your clientele, target new clients, identify clients who are due in for services, and a lot more! These specific features should lead to increased revenue and customer satisfaction.

However, the reality is that the software or POS application is a "supporting cast" under the overall marketing umbrella. Other marketing and branding methods not handled by the software or POS application, include, but are not limited to: social media, search engine optimization, and website development. You will need more advanced/strategic campaigns for promoting your brand, offerings, and specials that extend beyond the capabilities and features of the software or POS application.

As a new business owner, you may find yourself inundated with everything from staffing, to furniture, to software, and POS application research. You're only one person and you can't do everything yourself. In addition, your budget may not allow you to hire an in-house marketing specialist/director to help take care of these essential marketing tasks.

This is a perfect opportunity to seek out referrals or recommended business partners from your software or POS application. Leverage their expertise and years of experience within the industry to find out what works and what doesn't. The level of commitment to the industry by the software or POS application vendor should be further emphasized by the affiliates they recommend for marketing and advertising support.

THE GOOD, THE BAD & THE UGLY

(Brought to you by barbershop and salon owners and other industry leaders)

Anna Martin Craig

"Our salon software does everything but cut our client's hair. It is amazing. We would be lost without it. I couldn't imagine going back to paper books. We can keep record of every little thing we've ever done. It makes our job so much easier. My salon accountant is my mom, my other owner. So I definitely trust her. It makes a perfect partnership."

Mr. Ray's Barbershop

"The software we use does many things. I don't know what we would do without it. In today's world, most guys don't carry cash. I use it for expediting the sale, tracking clients, how and what they spend each time they come in, and who my best salespeople are each day, week, and month. It also keeps a recording of tips. This makes it easier for me when it's tax time."

CHAPTER 23

Credit Card Processing—Selecting the Right Partner

Written by Guy Wadas, National Sales Director, Integrity Payment Systems

Understanding credit card processing and knowing how to leverage its advantages can have a dramatic, profitable impact for barbershop owners. Choosing the wrong credit card processor or not understanding the best way to structure your processor agreement can be a constant monthly drain on your business.

Most businesses—no matter how large or small—make very small profits on a percentage basis. Knowing how to increase your profits—even by a percentage point or two—can provide the difference between "getting by" and enjoying a business which provides you with the lifestyle you want.

Following is an overview of the reasons to accept credit cards, the costs and benefits of credit card processing, how to select the right processor, and what questions to ask before signing any agreement. At the end of the chapter, we will also provide a list of unique programs offered to barbershop owners by one credit card processing company, including a free assessment of your current costs.

Why Accept Credit Cards?

For some barbershop owners, operating on a strictly cash basis seems like the least costly way to operate. No processing fees, no equipment to buy—and, it seems clean and simple. In fact, in the early 1990s, more than 80 percent of the money coming into hair, beauty, and grooming businesses was in the form of cash. Now, however, that number has flipped and more than 80 percent of the money comes in through credit or checking/debit cards. Why the switch? It's all about convenience for your clients and the potential additional profits for your barbershop.

Everything has a cost. Identifying the cost of credit card processing on the balance sheet is easy to do. What is not easy is to identify the cost of NOT accepting credit cards in your business. Several studies have shown that clients are willing to spend more when paying with credit than when paying with cash. In fact, when J.C. Penney Company, Inc. started to accept credit cards in its stores several years ago, it found that the average transaction for credit clients was $50 compared to cash transactions of only $20. People are not carrying cash these days; instead, they want the convenience of paying with credit or debit cards.

Barbershop owners can capitalize on this by offering products to their clients as well as add-on services. When paying with credit, clients are much more likely to purchase a service package, gift certificates/cards, as well as retail. Walk-in clients are also likely to prefer to pay with credit by the same 80/20 ratio. Referring these clients to a nearby ATM machine sends the message that you are more concerned about your convenience rather than making it easier for your clients to do business with you. Many will not come back to an establishment that does not accept payment via credit/debit card. The cost of NOT accepting credit may be the loss of sales in additional products and services over months and years, and you could lose the 80 percent of clients who no longer prefer to pay with cash.

If it makes sense to accept credit and debit card payments in your barbershop, how do you make sure you do this in a way that is best for you, rather than your bank or a third-party processor?

Choosing the Right Processor

Your local bank may provide credit processing either directly or through a third-party processor. You can also contract directly with a processor like Integrity Payment Systems. Who you choose for this important process can make a huge difference in your bottom-line profits.

Most local banks outsource this service to a third party that has an agreement or arrangement with the bank. A few national banks process credit transactions themselves. Regardless, you need to ask several key questions in order to make sure you have the best program for your business.

If the processing is outsourced, it is likely the customer service will also be outsourced. That can create a very frustrating situation should you have a problem or question. Look for a full-service credit card processor that handles not only the sales, but also the back-end processing, customer service, and other functions. They will be the most secure when it comes to protecting your clients' sensitive credit card information. They will also be the most responsive should you ever have an issue.

Is the Lowest Rate Always Best?

Most processors will quote a rate for processing transactions and position a rate that is one of the lowest rates available. What they do not tell you about are the additional fees involved, including a substantial cancellation or early-termination fee designed to keep you locked into the contract even after you find a better provider. Low rates can be deceiving. Be sure you understand all the terms in the contract.

You want to get to a number called "total cost" or "effective rate." That number includes not only the low rate, but all of the add-on charges, fees, and other costs. The effective rate is the number that matters, not the initial rate.

Card companies such as Visa, MasterCard, Discover, and American Express set different rates for different cards, industries, and customers. These rates are called interchange. They are numerous, and to further complicate the picture, these rates range anywhere from a zero percentage rate with a small per-item fee, to levels that include a percentage rate greater than three percent with large per-item fees. Unless you are working with a company that specializes in the hair, beauty, and grooming industry, it is unlikely you will be able to obtain the most favorable rates for your business. In fact, you will most likely be quoted the same rates and pricing structures as the car repair shop down the street. One size does not fit all, and one rate for all businesses is not going to fit either.

Integrity Payment Systems has been monitoring the flow of transactions for the hair, beauty, and grooming industry for many years. Your barbershop will not be lost in their system, as they have a dedicated in-house division that tracks and examines the interchange rates specifically for thousands of salon/barbershop businesses across the nation. Acquiring this data has enabled the exceptional ability to verify that barbershop owners are being charged correctly and at the best rate for their specific business.

Does the Processor Understand the Barbershop Business?

Another indicator of an appropriate credit card processor for your business is how well the company understands the barbershop business and the challenges you face. If the credit card processor is endorsed by respected industry partners such as Redken, Pureology, L'Oreal Professional, Matrix, Mizani, and others, it is a good sign that they offer a mix of services and products which will be most appropriate for your business. Other endorsements to look for include the Summit Salon Business Center (the largest salon consulting firm), The Salon Professional Academy schools, State Beauty Supply, RDA ProMart distributor stores, and Salon Centric (the largest salon product distribution hub in America).

Beyond the endorsements of industry professionals, barbershop owners should be aware of additional programs and services tailored exclusively to the owner's business needs. For example, Integrity Payment Systems (which is endorsed by the abovementioned salon industry companies and more) has created four unique services to help create a successful and profitable business. Barbershop owners control each of these services and direct each of the percentages, which include:

1. Auto-Save: a system which helps barbershop owners build an emergency fund automatically by separating a small percentage of each transaction into their savings account.

2. Pay-Fast Bill Payment: helps barbershop owners automatically stay current with bills by directing a percentage of each transaction to payment of key vendors.

3. Pay-Fast Debt Elimination: eliminates debt by systematically directing a portion of each transaction to pay creditors.

4. B.O.B.: helps barbershop owners accurately anticipate costs, revenue, and other budget items to plan for profitability.

Because barbershop owners are part of the Integrity team, the company was able to look at issues affecting owners and devise helpful solutions which leverage the credit card processing technology.

Better management of credit and debit processing can add new clients and increase the average ticket size. With the help of special tools, barbershop owners can save for the future, pay off debts, and budget for improved profitability.

THE GOOD, THE BAD & THE UGLY

(Brought to you by barbershop and salon owners and other industry leaders)

Chris Pearson, HQ Barbers, Tampa, FL

"You can save thousands of dollars and tons of hidden fees. You always need to shop your provider to keep them honest."

CHAPTER 24

Choosing a Phone System for Your Barbershop

Small-business phone systems are available in a variety of configurations, offering an ever-growing range of features and benefits that will help you communicate more efficiently with your clients and staff. The days of running out and buying a phone are a thing of the past. Choosing the right phone system for your business today is a more daunting task.

The newest and most advanced technology best suited for your barbering business runs on an Internet Protocol (IP) network. The network can be used to connect your home, office, and employees' devices and information resources.

When evaluating what type of phone system and service to use, you will first need to decide what works in your business environment, and how important it is for you to be able to reach certain key employees at work and while at home.

Understanding the Needs of Your Business

The right small-business phone system can give your staff the tools they need to be more efficient. Does the barbershop need the phone to ring on multiple devices? Is it important to be able to have your home office as an extension on the system? Is it necessary to have a phone in the barbershop's office, dispensary area, or break room?

It's important to know what your barbershop needs so you can choose wisely among the many features offered. Many of the features may be overkill for your barbershop. With technology advancing at such a quick rate, the value of choosing the right system can make communicating with your staff so much easier. Some offer options that give you more flexibility and mobility and allow you to connect via your phone system from home or while on the road. Among the many features and capabilities to consider:

- Mobile softphones—for using your computer as a phone. Great for booking appointments.
- Videoconferencing—a great tool for having a meeting while out of town or having an education class.
- Paging and Intercom—wonderful tool for letting one of your team members know that their next client has arrived or that they have a phone call.
- Presence Technology—gives your front desk person the ability to see who is available at any given time, as well as the best way to reach them.
- Wireless IP Phones—enabling staff to access data and be easily accessible when in the break or supply room.
- Unified messaging—providing notifications by email, text message, or voicemail. Great for keeping in touch with your barbershop, staff, and clients.

Cutting-Edge Technology

Your new small-business phone system can help your employees do things that once were not possible. It will change the way you do business. Being in touch enables you to make business decisions on the spot. You know when there is a problem and you can quickly connect to your key people in an instant. The benefits of using an IP system are listed below.

1. Your front desk professionals never have to leave their area to communicate with staff.
2. Messages can be forwarded directly to your mobile or home phone.
3. Messages can also be forwarded to your email.
4. Your staff does not have to leave a client's side when they need to ask you a question.
5. You can set up a conference call with your entire staff, communicating in real time.
6. The system is wireless.
7. Studies have shown that by using an IP system, you will save up to 40 percent on your phone bill and up to 90 percent on international calls.
8. You can get reports and monitor calls on each line in your barbershop.
9. Flexibility when adding more users to your system.
10. All of your employees can be tied together.

The benefits of having the IP system in your new or remodeled barbershop will outweigh the older, traditional phone systems. You can now be connected to your business from anywhere in the world. Imagine that you are on vacation and staying at a hotel with a high-speed Internet connection. You can now receive and make calls through your softphone just like you were sitting in your barbershop. The person you are talking to will have no idea where you are calling from while conducting business.

Don't just improve the way you do business, you must explore technology and be open-minded to change. These new phone systems will allow you better time management, increased functionality, and improved productivity in your barbershop with a lower cost.

CHAPTER 25

Why Your Business Name Is Important

Selecting a name for your barbershop is not easy. A name reflects more than the identity of your company. It tells clients who you are, what you do, and more than a little about how you do it. Your clients should be able to get an idea of what to expect when they walk through your door. If you do it right, your name will differentiate you from your peers, pique your clients' interest, and invite further investigation.

What's in a name? A lot, when it comes to small business success. The right name can make your company the talk of the town—the wrong one can doom you into obscurity and failure. If you're smart, you will put as much effort into naming your barbershop as you did with coming up with the idea to open one. Ideally, your name should convey the expertise, value, and uniqueness of the product or services you plan to offer.

How you come up with a name is largely a matter of personal preference. Some people want to include their own name as part of their barbershop name. Others may use the location of the shop or even something that reflects the history of the town or building. There are many different ways to choose names. We have come up with some effective elements that will help you with the process.

Tell Us Who You Are

Your name should reflect your identity. It is an essential aspect of branding. You will be promoting this name, getting it in front of as many eyes as possible, as often as possible. How do you want the public to think of you and your barbershop?

For some, that means integrating your name or the names of your children into your business. We don't recommend this because if you want to sell your barbershop in the future, the name is synonymous with you and you only. If you leave the business, the name dies when you leave. The potential buyer may and should view this as a big problem. It would be better to be known as the "The Guy Cave and Barbershop" than "Pat's Guy Cave and Barbershop."

Tell Us What You Do

It is incredible how many business names give little, if any, indication of what services they actually provide. Try to choose a name that you want your barbershop to be identified with. If you're starting a barbershop that is for new, progressive cuts, then you want a name that conveys innovation and talent, something different or out of this world. Doing so will also set the stage for new barbers or stylists who may be looking for a change of job and a fresh start. By letting your name tell prospective clients and employees what you do, your name will open doors you may never believe possible.

Just Another Barbershop

Your name is the first opportunity to tell customers how you are different from the competition. That can be done by emphasizing what makes you different, pinpointing what aspect of your products and services can't be found anywhere else, or what you do better than the barbershop down the street.

Pique Clients' Interest

Creating client interest is an art and a science. Think carefully about your target market. What qualities of your services are of great importance to your clients? What type of words would appeal to that client? The words in your name should be inviting, approachable, and make clients feel like they will be comfortable in your place of business.

Let's Do It

What do you need to help you come up with a name? Find a quiet room, thesaurus, and writing pad. Jot down as many ideas the come to mind or words that you like. Then, call on your friends and family for some good feedback. The process shouldn't take you more than a few hours. Here are some quick tips on getting started:

- Brainstorm: Think about how you want people to feel when they hear your name.
- Relate: Think about related words and phrases that evoke the feelings you want.
- Experiment: Start playing with combinations of various words and phrases or unique spellings for words.
- Reflect: Review your list and give some thought to each name and how you feel when you hear it.

- Communicate: Go over it with family and friends and have them give their gut feeling on what they think.
- Prioritize: Throw out the names you hate and only keep the ones you like.
- Check domain names: See if the name is available for a domain name for your website through www.whois.com.
- Have fun: Remember that this name will be with you for a long time.

THE GOOD, THE BAD & THE UGLY

(Brought to you by barbershop and salon owners and other industry leaders)

The Gents Place, Von Jackson, Frisco, TX

"We wanted something simple and masculine, yet flexible enough to allow a world-class brand to be born. The Gents Place fulfilled all of those criteria, and the name has already allowed us to expand into a 'lifestyle' brand that goes way beyond men's grooming."

The Ultimate Barber Lounge, Tone McGill, Charlotte, NC

"I believe that the only word that could define the quality of our service and professionalism that we offer to our clients is ULTIMATE. The word Lounge is included to depict the relaxed feeling of being in our barbershop which is also supported by our choice in furniture and décor."

Chris Pearson, HQ Barbers Tampa Florida

"Your name must be easy to remember and identify what your business is about."

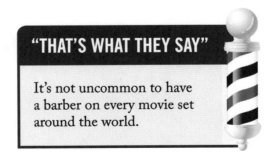

"THAT'S WHAT THEY SAY"

It's not uncommon to have a barber on every movie set around the world.

CHAPTER 26

Business Insurance—Why You Need It!

Business insurance protects you and your business from liability, accidents, or damage. Barbershop owners trying to save a few dollars when opening up their business make the crucial mistake of forgoing business insurance. Good luck and positive thinking will not protect you, your staff, and clients from losses. Unfortunately, bad things happen even to the most conscientious owners.

Factual Scenarios: This Can Happen To You

- You arrive at work to find your shampoo shuttle leaked all over your brand-new hardwood floors and the entire floor is buckled.
- A client slips in your shampoo area and breaks his ankle.
- One of your clients has a heart attack while having his hair cut.
- One of your employees leaves the coffee maker on and it burns down your barbershop and building.
- A member of your staff cuts a client while giving a shave or haircut.
- You suddenly need carpal tunnel surgery and will not be able to work for two months.

As you can see, there are many different reasons why you will need insurance for you and your barbershop. Different types of insurance can cover the contents of your barbershop, your health, liability, and your property. Having insurance for everything can be quite expensive. Let's focus on what will suit your needs when first opening a barbershop.

Liability Insurance

What has the world come to? America was once known as the "promised land." A person could come and build a business empire from the ground up and have a fresh start. The United States offers this opportunity which is unlikely anywhere else in the world.

We are now known for something else. America is known for lawsuits. Lawsuits are like baseball, apple pie, and hamburgers—it's the American way. Allow us to add one more thing to the list—lawyers. You need to protect your business from legal expenses, settlements or judgments, and lawsuits. Liability policies cover business losses for payments to victims of bodily injury or property damage caused by your business. This insurance will also cover medical expenses to victims, attorney fees, and expenses associated with legal proceedings. General liability is a must-have for your daily business operation.

Business Property Insurance

Business property insurance covers your business in case of unforeseen damage or loss to your building, inventory, or equipment. That means even if the neon sign hanging out in front of your barbershop shorts out in a storm, you would be covered to have it fixed or replaced. Business property insurance coverage extends to items such as: laptops, phones, furniture, and valuable documents.

Types of Business Property Insurance

According to the National Association of Insurance Commissioners, there are three kinds of business property insurance:

1. **Basic**—covers damages from natural disasters such as fire, storms, and explosions.
2. **Broad**—covers the basic damages, plus other unforeseen events, such as a riot, that leaves the barbershop in shambles.
3. **Special**—the most comprehensive form of business insurance. It covers basic and broad, plus all the direct physical loss that is included in your policy.

Business Property Insurance for Owners Who Rent Their Store

If you rent your store, don't assume that the landlord is responsible for losses to your business and property. While the building itself is most likely covered, your inventory, computers, barbershop equipment, and other property related to your business are not. You must have business property insurance to cover the contents of your barbershop.

If you have financed your barbershop equipment, computers, phone system, or any other equipment, the bank or finance company will make it mandatory that you have personal property insurance on everything you financed through them.

Key Person Insurance

Most small businesses, and almost all start-up businesses, depend on the talents or abilities of a few key people. If you are a "one-man band" or rely on just a few people for the success of your business, your business could fail if something should happen to you or any of your key people. Key person insurance is a way for businesses to insure against business interruption if a key person becomes injured or ill.

Worker's Compensation Insurance

Worker's Compensation coverage is required by state, local, and federal law. If you have employees, you will have no choice about it. The fact of the matter is, if one of your employees gets hurt at work, whether it's your fault or not, you want to be prepared for a lawsuit. Workers' Compensation Insurance will cover hospital bills, attorney fees, lawsuit awards, and lost wages.

Buying Insurance

Start by finding three insurance companies in your area. Explain exactly what kind of business you will be opening and how many employees you will have. You also need to have a list of the contents (equipment) that will be used in your place of business. Explain to the agent or broker what types of services you will offer. They may feel you need additional coverage. There are a few variables to consider when purchasing your insurance: price, coverage offered, specialization of insurance company, reputation of the insurance company, and the size of the deductible.

Price

Settling on the lowest price is not always the best choice. If one company is much cheaper than another, they may be leaving out a large portion of your coverage. Ask questions, read the policies, and compare.

Coverage

Negotiate more coverage in all aspects. No policy is cast in stone. The worst they can say is no. When it comes to insurance, it doesn't hurt to be over-insured.

Specialization of the Company

Each industry and business has its own risk. When picking an insurance company, make sure they specialize in small businesses and have insured other barbershops or similar businesses, such as hair salons.

Reputation of the Insurance Company

Try to work with an insurance company in your area. They may be on "Main Street" in your town. It also makes sense to look online to see if they are in good financial shape. You can check with "Best Insurance Reports." If the company is not rated from an A+ to a B, you should look elsewhere for your insurance.

Deductible

The deductible is one of the most important parts of your policy. A higher deductible will mean lower insurance costs, but it will also increase how much you have to pay for any losses you may have.

Whatever you do, remember that whoever is writing your insurance policies is doing so because he or she earns commissions on these policies. Your interests and theirs may not always agree. It means that you should shop around, negotiate, and always be on the lookout for a better deal.

As a business owner, you know the value of protecting yourself, your family, your staff, and your clients. Be sure to purchase an insurance policy that will safeguard all aspects of your investment.

THE GOOD, BAD & THE UGLY

(Brought to you by barbershop and salon owners and other industry leaders)

Marissa's House of Style

"We had a fire in the salon. Most of the salon was destroyed. I had the right insurance company. A client's husband was my insurance agent. He guided me through the whole crisis. I was able to rebuild my salon from the ground up. My salon is now more beautiful than before. Thank the Lord I had the right insurance. I was blessed."

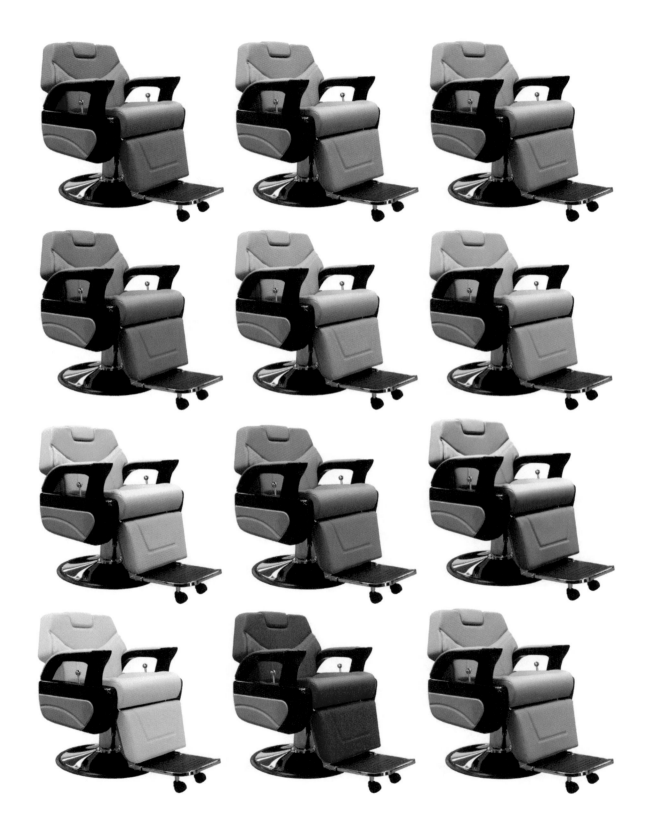

CHAPTER 27

The Color of Money—What Color Is Your Business?

As a barbershop owner, you have a meaningful understanding of the color of money, but how about the color of your business? You must understand that the colors you choose for your business puts your clients in a buying mood or creates the wrong perception for your barbershop.

The power of colors stimulates our nervous system and evokes emotional states. The colors of the environment trigger feelings to the brain, causing various hormonal releases. You may have never thought that there is a science of colors. Colors have an impact on our body and mind. Big corporate businesses have been studying and using colors to influence buyers for many years. Market research specialists have applied their knowledge to many businesses around the world to help business owners leverage every angle to enhance retail buying. Color is often called the "silent salesperson." Color must immediately attract the holder's eye, convey the message of what the business is about, create a brand identity, and most importantly, help make the sale. That's right the colors you choose can put your male clients in a relaxed atmosphere and a buying mood. As you might guess, pink isn't a favorite color for men. Blue, green, and black are generally the colors that men like most. The colors traditionally considered masculine are good choices for your barbershop business.

You may be thinking, "Wow, this all seems crazy, too much information, brain overload, is this really important?" Yes, it sure is. Let's forget the science and find out why the right colors will show you the "green" (money) in your barbershop.

The Meaning of Colors & Your Business

The meaning of colors varies depending on one's culture, race, gender, and even age. It's not just the selection of colors in general, but also which colors to use with your target client. Much of the human reaction to color is subliminal and clients in your barbershop will generally not be aware of the persuasive effects of color.

We have listed the colors below that have cool patterns, favorite sport team colors, deep rich tones that will ultimately make your male clients feel comfortable, relaxed, and ready to hang out and spend money at your place of business.

Reinvent the Color Wheel to Your Advantage

Black: Power, elegance, Secretive, sexy. Black is beautiful. The color can target your heightened market or be used in youth marketing. If you are looking to add sexy, big, strong, and proud, then use black as an accent color or use it on the walls where you may want to hang pictures or sports memorabilia.

Green: Green is the second color on the list of men's favorites. Green is a relaxing, cool color that signifies growth, and money! It promotes a clean environment as well as stability. There are many shades of green that can be suited to your barbershop. We find that men like a deep green color. This represents the color of football, baseball, and any outside sport's turf. It also just generally reminds them of the outdoors. If they sit in an office all day, this deep green color can renew most anyone. A wall of green with a big flat screen TV or football/baseball pictures would give a classic, sporty look.

Blue: Blue is the favorite color of men of all ages. Blue signifies authority, intelligence, and the military. Blue stands for trust and loyalty. What more could you want in a color? Women also find blue to be one of their favorite colors.

Subconsciously, blue reflects faithfulness, honesty, and integrity. Aren't those the three most important things when you are in business? Wouldn't it be nice if every one of your clients looked at your business and you, as the owner, that way?

There are many different shades of blue. Whether it's a blue uniform, a blue suit, or a few walls in your barbershop, it's a great color. You can't lose with the color blue. We urge you to use the color blue in your place of business anywhere you can.

White: Pure, clean, youthful. It's a neutral color that can imply purity, cleanliness, peace, innocence, winter, snow, and, of course, marriage. White might be right for many businesses, but the barbershop needs to have more of a rugged, stately sports-like atmosphere. Leave the pure colors for home, not the barbershop.

In the end, when deciding your color choice for the barbershop, remember, colors have meaning. The clients you attract may reflect what colors you choose. Is your barbershop located in an older market or a younger age group? All of this will help you choose what colors best fit your market and clientele.

What about these other colors for furniture or accents in your barbershop?

○ **Bronze:** Strong and masculine yet sophisticated.

○ **Burgundy:** For years, the color was dated. But, it's in and fresh again.

○ **Turquoise:** Great for a billiard room or when used with rich woods on a barbering workstation.

○ **Camel:** It's a flattering color, yet masculine. Nice touch for the walls of your shop.

○ **Moroccan Red:** The red of the British Military or the famous Red Coats will make any barbershop "pop" with brilliance.

THE GOOD, THE BAD & THE UGLY

(Brought to you by barbershop and salon owners and other industry leaders)

Stand Tall Barbers, Dallas, TX

"We are in the heart of Dallas. What city is more proud of their football team? The shop stands tall and proud for the Dallas Cowboys. My walls are silver with black and white accents. My barber chairs were reupholstered with a Dallas Star on the seats. We have Dallas memorabilia everywhere, with five big flat-screen TVs. I have every sport magazine available for my clients. They love coming here and I love coming to work."

Chris Pearson, HQ Barbers, Tampa, FL

"Identify the look and feel you like, we took "Starbucks" as our guide. We knew that Starbucks created an atmosphere for men and women could spend money and relax in a comfortable environment. Why recreate the wheel, when you have a proven design that works. We chose this for our barbershops."

CHAPTER 28

The Importance of Signage

Signage in front or on top of your storefront is your billboard. Your sign is the single most effective way to communicate what your business is, what you do, what you sell, and what you offer. Business signage is a representation of you and your business.

Clients attracted by business signage include those who are just passing by or those who are new to the neighborhood. A sign is the most effective way to reach this group of potential clients.

If your business site is in an area that is not easily accessible, then your sign is the only thing that can communicate to people who are driving by your barbershop. The barbershop that is located off of a freeway can use a high-rise sign to attract some of the people traveling on nearby roads and expressways.

NOTE

There is no better "signage" than a good, old-fashioned barber pole in front of your barbershop or men's grooming salon to let people know you offer barbering services. Be sure to incorporate a one into your plans for signage. If it has worked for hundreds of years, don't "recreate the wheel."

Signage—A Way of Life

Ever since anyone can remember, signs have been used as an effective marketing tool for different occasions, events, and business purposes. From the moment you leave your house, you will see one sign or another within five minutes. It makes you wonder why we don't get information overload from signage. There is a reason why some signs have an impact on you and others just blend in with the environment. Sign overload is a way of life, but making a sign with lasting impact on the client should be your goal. Your sign must effectively touch the emotion and life of your client.

All Shapes, Sizes, & Designs

The big question you are going to have is: What type of sign do you put on your location and what material should you use? Materials can include PVC, neon, or steel/aluminum. Signage designs can suite a variety of budget, design, landlord, and city requirements.

Remember, business signage does not have to be just metal or large neon. You can utilize all kinds of modern technologies and inventions to effectively brand and promote your business, such as:

- Plastics that do not rust, where you can interchange graphics as products and/or models change for haircare products.
- Weatherproof digital banner signs that go on your personal car or store windows.

When designing your sign, it must be easy to read and placed where it can be seen.

City or Town Requirements

Each city or town will have different requirements and restrictions, such as: height, placement, colors, or material. Your city or town may not allow signs in the windows and/or obstructions on the lawn in front of your location. To find out what is acceptable, contact your local building department and request the current guidelines.

The cost of your signs will vary depending on what product the sign is made out of and if it is illuminated. The least expensive sign is aluminum and steel, ranging from $2,000 to $4,000. An illuminated block letter sign will range from $3,000 to $7,000, depending on the size and number of letters. Graphics for your store windows will depend on the size and layout and how many colors, but will range between $500 and $1,000. Weatherproof sign graphics for your car will cost between $1,000 for half of your car and $2,000 for a full-size car or van.

NOTE

The landlord may want you to follow the same design as everyone else in the plaza. Read your lease carefully for the requirements and restrictions, such as size and type, and whether window signs and neon are allowed.

✓ CHECK IT OUT

When deciding upon what type of sign or where you will place it, have you thought about these very important items?

Check off the questions below as you answer them.

○ Will your town and landlord allow you to put a barber pole outside your business? If not, you may have to get creative. Use your window space to prominently display a barber pole from the inside of your barbershop. Or, incorporate a barber pole in the artwork for your barbershop sign.

○ Will your sign be visible from all directions?

○ Will your sign attract new clients?

○ Will your sign "brand" your barbershop?

○ Is your sign appealing and legible?

○ Can you put your logo on the sign?

○ Does it need to be illuminated?

○ Will it block your windows?

○ Is there any obstruction or part of the building that limits its size?

CHAPTER 29

The Facelift—Remodeling Your Barbershop

"The road to success is always under construction."

—Lily Tomlin

This might be the best time to start planning an image upgrade and a barbershop remodel. By remodeling your barbershop, you can totally change your image. Many things have changed in the way we conduct business in the barbershop environment. The once-loyal client is looking to better manage work and family through value, better customer service, and the ability to shop closer to home. These changes in the way people do business will have far-reaching effects that won't disappear overnight.

The marketing of your barbershop, your budgeting skills, and how you manage clients and staff has to adapt for business survival. You can't expect your business to strive and do well without changing your image and brand to be in sync with the times. The current appearance of your barbershop may look dated, tired, and even dirty to your clients. Once your barbershop reaches this point, it may be too late. The longer you wait to make changes the more it will cost you in construction and improvements to catch up to your competition.

While the thought of investing in a remodel can be overwhelming, don't let your fears get the best of you. If things are slow, use this time to focus on a remodel and a new image for your barbershop business.

Cost, Budget, & Value

You have committed to moving forward with the project, but how do you figure out what you want to spend? How much will it cost to move a wall, rip out the old floor, and buy all new furniture and equipment? What should you expect to spend? How do you set an appropriate budget? How long should you expect to take before all this pays you back? How can you maximize your return on investment?

This section lays out the foundation and factors regarding how much to spend on your build-out and new barbering furniture/equipment.

Cost

Breaking it down to the simplest terms, the cost is a function of the materials you will need for your build-out, the time, the labor for the contractors to complete the work, and the new equipment you will be purchasing.

Budget

We all want the best of everything, but most of us have champagne tastes with a beer budget. Your list of needs and wants may exceed your ability to foot the bill. While the cost of the renovation will vary due to many different things, like how extensive the remodel and what type of furniture/equipment you choose, you still have to establish a budget.

Deciding on your budget is based on some critical information. Generally, it depends on your demographics, how much you charge for services, and what type of clients your barbershop attracts. You also need to know what you can afford as a monthly payment if financing is needed. You should factor in what you have put aside in cash for the project.

Return on Investment

How do you know if your investment is going to pay off? How long will it take to recoup your remodeling dollars?

There is a particular rule of thumb for return of investment in remodeling your barbershop business. Statistics show that normally you can expect an increase of business of about 20 percent in the first year of your remodel. This increase would come from new clients that have never visited your barbershop before the remodel.

Your current staff and existing clients will have the benefit of now working at and visiting the hottest barbershop in the area. The fact that you are keeping your current clients and not losing staff to competitors down the street is a big factor you must weigh into your calculations when figuring your overall return on investment.

What's Your Budget?

There are many ways to change the look of a barbershop. The cost does not have to be in the tens of thousands. Whether your budget is $1,000, $20,000, or $100,000, most changes will significantly increase business within the first year of the remodel. This will keep your barbershop looking fresh and ahead of your competition. Your clients will appreciate it and so will your staff.

Remodeling Your Barbershop on a Tight Budget

Mr. Clean

The best way to make your barbershop look fresh and give it a new look is with a deep clean. Roll up your sleeves and put on a fresh set of gloves and get down to business or hire a commercial cleaning service. We suggest a commercial cleaning service—whether it's once or twice a year or even once a quarter. They will get into every corner of your business and wipe away years of grime. This will give your barbershop a fresh appearance that your clients will notice. Plus, a nice fresh floor waxing will make any barbershop look new.

Replace every bulb in your barbershop. Light levels in regular and florescent bulbs tend to be less bright or give off a brownish glare after a couple of years. Changing your bulbs will brighten up the way everything in your shop looks. Light brings life!

Bring in New Products

Changing your barbershop doesn't always have to be with a paint brush and a hammer. Bring in new products, change your shelving, and show your clients you are committed to the grooming industry by introducing them to cutting-edge grooming products.

New Services

Men are also looking for ways to look and feel better. Expanding your services is a great way to keep your current clients or attract new ones. Here is a list of services that may work for you.

- Shoeshine
- Pedicures
- Manicures
- Facials
- Shaving
- Color or Hair Treatments
- Hair Replacement

> **TIP**
>
> Many barber chairs accumulate a build-up of different types styling products and normal cleaners do not work. A great cleaning product to use is "mineral spirits," which doesn't hurt vinyl and loosens the spray build-up. Before you apply this, please confirm that your chair material is actually vinyl, NOT LEATHER!

Look Up

If your ceiling is dirty or has water stains, either give it a coat of paint or change out the stained ceiling tiles (we will talk more about ceiling tiles later in this chapter). The worst thing in the barbershop business is when you are getting your hair shampooed and you look up and see a water-stained ceiling. This is a sign of true neglect in a barbershop.

Your "Door" to Success

The first and last thing your staff and clients see when walking into your barbershop is your front door. Your front door should always be clean. If it is wood, give it a fresh coat of paint. If it's full glass, you may want to put your name, logo, and hours on the door. This inexpensive way to make a noticeable change!

The First Step

Designer/Architect

To find out the costs of this endeavor, we recommend you bring in a specialist in the industry. Several companies specialize in the hair, beauty, and barbering industry and can offer their expertise in layout, furniture, and equipment (see CHAPTER 14: Designing & Space-Planning for Your Barbershop). They need to come to the barbershop, see what you want to change, and discuss the look you want to create. You will pay a design fee; but, if you are doing a complete makeover, we recommend it highly. They have the knowledge that you need and can give you advice on prioritizing your remodeling steps.

Contractors

Usually, you bring in a contractor only for extensive changes. But, every situation is different, depending on how much remodeling you want to do. You may only want to paint and change the floor. For this type of work, you may not need a general contractor. Take two steps: bring in a contractor and get a complete price on everything you want to do. Next, bring in separate subcontractors: a plumber, electrician, floor specialist, and a drywall team to get separate prices on your projects. That will start to give you an idea of costs.

If you are just replacing the barber furniture, your contractor/installation costs should be minimal.

Create a Spreadsheet

Below is a spreadsheet with a sample of all the costs you may incur for your remodel. We recommend you fill it out and get a complete breakdown of what you want to do. It is a good guideline to start seeing your costs and what you want to spend on your remodeling project.

Construction Breakdown		Furniture Breakdown	
Plumbing		Barber chairs	
Electrical		Dryer chairs	
Drywall		Shampoo units	
Painting		Shampoo cabinet	
Flooring		Pedicure chairs	
Construction demolition		Manicure stations	
Signage		Stools	
Telephone		Barbering stations	
Computer		Color stations	
Window treatment		Color chairs	
Furniture installation		Dispensary	
Furniture demolition		Color lab	
Architect's plans		Reception desk	
Permits		Shoeshine bench	
Garbage removal		Retail area	
		Reception furniture	
TOTAL		**TOTAL**	

Painting Changes the Look with a Small Price Tag

When opening a barbershop or remodeling an existing one, you will be faced with a major obstacle. What is the first thing you should do that fits your budget, but will have the biggest impact?

Of course, you want to rip out everything and start from scratch. We all want to have the best of everything when we own a business. The fact is you just might not be able to afford it.

What is the one thing that can instantly change the look and appearance of your barbershop once it is done? The answer is new, fresh paint. The best part about painting is that you don't always have to hire a professional to do the work. Most of us are capable of painting. It's usually easy to find family, friends, and maybe few employees to assist with the project.

Consider changing the colors. We write about colors for your barbershop in CHAPTER 27: The Color of Money—What Color Is Your Business? Changing the color will give you and your clients the greatest sense of immediate change and satisfaction. Follow these tips to decrease effort and cost involved with painting:

- Make sure you have enough drop cloths to cover everything.
- Tape off places that you don't want to get paint on. (It will take a while to do, but cleanup of unwanted paint takes hours.)
- Buy enough paint. (You don't want to run out in the middle of the project to buy more paint.)
- Make sure you buy paint you can wipe and clean (semi-gloss or eggshell finish).
- Paint the ceilings first, then the walls.
- Don't buy cheap brushes and rollers.
- Use top-grade paint.

If painting is not your thing and you just don't have the time, hire it out. You can search on Google and/or Yahoo for painters in your area. Listed below are the two most popular websites to find painters:

www.localpainterquotes.com

www.paintingnetworx.com

How Painters Determine What They Charge

Commercial painting contractors use several aspects to determine the formula for your project. The cheapest price you will get is on an empty space that is new construction; the most expensive is on an older building and/or restoration project. The factors listed below will help you understand how the project will be quoted and priced:

- How much barber furniture do they have to move?
- Do they have to work at night, around your schedule?

- How many windows and doors do they have to paint or cut in?
- How high are the ceilings? The higher the ceilings, the higher the quote. They will need ladders and scaffolding.
- Do you need a primer to cover old paint and stains?
- What type of repairs do they have to make to your walls?
- Trim (woodworking is measured by the linear foot for painting).
- Overall size of your space.

Ceiling Tiles

Changing ceiling tiles can be a quick fix and make the barbershop look new with a good paint job. Among residential ceiling choices, drop ceiling tiles are a preferred option. These durable tiles need little maintenance. However, drop ceiling tiles may develop a worn-out look over time. In such a scenario, you can simply paint them using a roller and vinyl paint to revitalize the look. To remove, paint, and replace your drop ceiling tiles, use the following information:

Step 1—Removing Drop Ceiling Tiles

Position a ladder against the drop ceiling. Prepare yourself with plastic gloves. Drop ceiling tiles are set within a frame or a tiling grid. Removing the tile without due care can harm the edges of the tile, making it unfit for reinstallation in its framework. The edges of the tile might be compacted with dust or grime. Use the tip of a flat screwdriver covered with cloth to scrape off the debris and push along the edges. Slightly push one end of the tile. You need to slide the tile along its frame. After pushing the tile forward, twist it to create an angle with the horizontal grid. Now, slide out the tile from its frame. If you find any loose wires, cover them with twist-on wire connectors or electrical tape.

Step 2—Examining Drop Ceiling Tile

Place the removed tile on a sheet of newspaper. Use a dry cloth to clean the tile. Examine the edges of the tile. If the edges are broken or if the surface of the tile is cracked in many places, you need to replace it. Otherwise, you can paint it.

Step 3—Painting Drop Ceiling Tile

Use a latex paint. You can use a paint roller or a paintbrush, depending upon the texture of the tile. Paint rollers are better for plain surfaces, while a brush helps to dab into the crevices of textured tiles. Use a latex paint with a color matching the surrounding drop ceiling tiles. It is best to protect the edges of the tile with masking tape when painting it, as painted edges might hamper the fitting of the tile into its designated slot. Allow the painted tile to dry for a few hours.

Step 4—Purchasing Replacement Drop Ceiling Tiles

Replacement drop ceiling tiles are available at hardware supply stores. Further, you can also contact the retailer from whom you purchased the tiles to request a replacement. It is better to purchase a couple of tiles for future replacements. The existing drop ceiling tile design may get outdated so having reserve tiles is a wise option.

Step 5—Installing Replacement/Painted Drop Ceiling Tile

Carry your replacement/painted tile up the ladder. Hold it in such a way that the finished/painted side is facing downward. Tilt the tile upward and into the grid. Allow nearly half of the ceiling tile to pass the grid's frame. Now, start to position the tile in a horizontal manner, ensuring that the tile's edges are tightly fitted along the frame.

Getting Started the Permit Way

If your barbershop is in operation, it is important to coordinate the remodel so you don't lose any business. If the job is large and permits are needed for the renovation, it is recommended that you do your remodel in stages.

For example, in changing your shampoo sinks, you need to pull out the old shampoo unit and cabinets, change the plumbing pipes, and install the new units. It is usually a two-day process. Once it's all done, then it's time to call the plumbing inspector in your city for inspection. Hopefully, the inspector will pass the plumbing work. If not, you can't use the sinks and won't be able to open until it is satisfactory to the inspector and is compliant to all county or city codes. That is just one inspection! What if you are trying to coordinate several inspections? It is a very difficult task. In this case, you are hiring a general contractor and it's his responsibility to make sure everything is done on time. The key is to tell him your priorities and let him coordinate these tasks with his subcontractors. Timing is everything.

Priorities—Plumbing

Most barbershops are open six days a week; so, it's important to have all of your furniture on hand or have your equipment supplier deliver it when needed. It might be a midnight install or your barbershop may have to close an extra day. With a traditional barbershop, usually there is a sink at every station. Therefore consider the amount of time needed to change the sinks and cabinets. Please refer to the following information for time and approximate cost.

If all of this is planned out well, you will avoid losing business or at least minimize the amount of time that you are closed for the remodel. You probably will pay a premium to have construction work being done during the evening; but, in most cases, you have no choice. First, you must tear out the old cabinets and sink units. If you are remodeling the dispensary and any pedicure units, all of this must be taken out as well.

Then, the installation begins. To install cabinets, such as a three-sink shampoo cabinet, the time it takes to professionally install it is usually four hours. Right behind that person will be a plumber to hook up all of the sinks. The average time to hook up each one is 1–3 hours, depending on the type. A freestanding sink unit and chair usually takes the longest. They must be bolted to the floor securely, which is the responsibility of the plumber. If he is a "one-man band," it could take a day and a half to secure and install three units; so, be prepared.

Here is a list of furniture and equipment with the length of time and cost to install (averages):

- Wall sink (cabinet installed by others): 1½ hours, including mounting the bracket: $100 each
- Freestanding backwash sink: 4 hours on average with bolting the unit to the floor: $250
- Pedicure Unit; 3 hours to install and assemble: $250
- Color lab sink or dispensary sink: 1½ hours to install: $175
- Facial room sink installation: $150
- Remodel existing bathroom: labor is $400 for new fixture installation
- Sink and cabinet combination: 3 hours labor: $225

These costs will help you estimate your construction budget. Prices may vary depending on the city or state you live in. These prices do not reflect any changes in your plumbing, such as adding another sink or moving all the hot and cold water lines over to accommodate another sink unit.

Hiring the Sub-Contractors

You are getting ready to remodel and have brought in an electrician, plumber, and a drywall contractor. How do you know they are charging a fair price? It is a tricky situation because you want a great price and you are on a very tight budget. How do you handle this?

Our rule of thumb is to bring in two to three tradesmen from the same field and have them bid on the same work. Have a complete checklist to hand to them for the bid. Let them know that it might be weekend work or in the evenings so that they price it accordingly. Plumbers and electricians get anywhere from $30 to $75 per hour, and on the weekends, maybe more. There may be a crew of two to three or just one. Get a complete price without the hourly breakdown. There are always some unforeseen situations and having a package deal is in your favor.

If you have three bids and two are about the same and one is considerably lower, you should be concerned. You may want to choose the lowest bidding contractor, but be careful! They either did not include something or did not charge enough for labor. The contractor might be the type that is spread very thin so your remodel will not be finished in a timely fashion. We would also check their references and recent work. See if they finished on time and on budget.

Permits—Plumbing

If permits are needed, here is the process. (Closing Saturday night – reopen Tuesday)

1. On Friday, call for a plumbing inspection with the city or county for Monday afternoon.

2. On Friday, deliver all new equipment/furniture concerning plumbing. If you don't have the room, pay a premium to get it delivered on Sunday morning. It depends on your barbershop space.

3. On Saturday—early evening—demolish all plumbing needed for the change.

4. On Sunday morning, bring in your cabinet company to install all furniture concerning plumbing.

5. Mid-Sunday morning, have your plumber come in and start prep work on all plumbing fixtures.

6. By noon Monday, the plumber finishes and you should be ready for the inspector.

7. By Tuesday morning, you will have passed inspection and reopened.

> **NOTE**
>
> Plan your plumbing time wisely because once your sinks are shut off, you are out of business until they are back up.

Priorities—Electric

Your electrical design in your newly bought barbershop could give you a few surprises, but not if you've read this chapter. One item that is often overlooked is the amount of power coming into your barbershop or the amount of amperage going to each barbering/styling station or other departments.

Here is the standard used in the industry. Some of these may not apply to your barbershop; it depends on the services that you offer:

*   Barbering station: Each station should have 10 amps of power with two stations on a 20-amp circuit breaker.

*   Dryer chair: Each dryer (behind-the-chair style) generally draws 8 amps, and it should have two dryers per 20-amp circuit.

*   Pedicure unit: This unit needs 20 amps on a ground fault interrupter (GFI) outlet.

*   Nail table: Each table should have 5 amps or two tables on a 10-amp circuit.

*   Reception desk: Recommended power for computers, credit card terminal, and miscellaneous items is 20 amps.

*   Color station: Not much power needed there; GFI outlet would be useful.

*   Color lab: Utility outlet and power for accessory lighting. Ready, Set, Go!

*   Retail area: This can vary, but with several retail units, 30-amp circuits are recommended for lighting.

*   Dispensary: Power for the washer, dryer, and hot water heater; these units usually need 220 volt power and require a lot of amperage. (Consult with your electrician.)

Several barbers working in the same area can trip the circuit breaker because too many appliances (three different clippers, a hot towel cabinet, and sterilizer) are on one circuit and it cannot handle the amount of power needed to support each station. The first thing to do is bring in an electrician and show him what you want to have done. If you are changing the barber stations, show him the new design. In a lot of cases, the electrical is in the wrong spot and has to move. You can also design your new station with the electrical in mind, so you don't have to move it. A design specialist, mentioned previously, would be able to identify that too.

Cost Breakout

Unless you are knowledgeable in electrical systems, the installation of outlets is not to be considered a "Do-it-Yourself" project. This is particularly true if new circuits need to be added to the electrical panel. Traditionally, installation is done by a professionally licensed electrician.

The costs for a project will include:

- Bringing electrical wiring and lighting to code: This is going to depend upon the amount of work required, but an electrician's average rate is from $65 to $85 per hour. Any given project might be priced on a per item basis or the electrician might simply craft a bid based on the number of tasks to be performed. Generally, it is recommended to have an electrician perform several installations on the same project to make it more cost effective.
- Installing standard outlets of 120 volts: Takes less than half an hour and usually costs around $100 each.
- Installing heavy-duty outlets of 220 to 240 volts: Takes less than half an hour and usually costs around $100 each.
- Installing grounded outlets for kitchens, bathrooms, and any places near water or moisture: Takes less than an hour and usually costs around $120 each.
- Installing a new circuit on the electrical panel and running the appropriate amount of conduit to the new location: This might take up to a full hour's time and costs around $185 each.
- Upgrading panel for heavy-duty outlets: Involves adding a 220 to 240-volt circuit, running conduit, and installing receptacle; this can take several hours and tends to cost around $650 for each addition.
- ▶ Remember all fixtures that you use must be UL (Underwriter's Laboratory) approved.

Wall-hanging station with no bottom cabinet:

This style station is widely used with an outlet usually located underneath and with the clippers located on the right of the station.

Wall station to the floor:

The outlet, again, is located in most cases on the right side of the station.

Continuous station on the wall

The design has all the wall-style units connected and the electric needs to be mounted on the face of the cabinet. It is accomplished by having the electric come from the wall with flexible BX (electrical) cable that is connected to the outlet located on the station.

Barber station with sink

This type of station is widely used in traditional barbershops and the outlet is usually located about 39 inches off the floor on the right side of the station. A quad outlet is recommended. There are two ways to accomplish this, one is to just mount a 4-prong outlet on the wall or have flexible BX cable coming out of the wall to attach to an outlet built in the station. The cable should come out of the wall at the height of 33 inches.

Freestanding back-to-back barber station

The unit needs electric either coming from the ceiling or the floor. Unless electric from the floor is already in place, you will have to cut the floor to get electric to it. Some owners just run a strip plug to the unit and keep the station a few feet from the wall. This is unsightly and presents a trip hazard, but it is an inexpensive option. The other alternative is to have the electric come from the ceiling, which usually has acoustical tile. The electric is covered with either hard conduit line or flexible BX cable. Most barbershops cover the line cosmetically.

Permits—Electric

If permits are needed, here is the process (Friday evening – reopen Tuesday morning). We recommend you close on Saturday because of the unusual amount of electrical work and coordination for this process.

1. On Friday, call for inspection for Monday afternoon.
2. If possible, deliver all furniture that requires electrical work for inspection on Friday. If there is no room in the barbershop for this, have it delivered on Saturday.
3. Friday evening, demolish all old cabinets and equipment/furniture concerning electric.
4. Start installing equipment/furniture Saturday and finish either that day or Sunday.
5. Electrician comes in Saturday afternoon to start working and to make sure he has the right supplies to handle the job.
6. Electrician works on all new connections, moving whatever electrical is needed and reconnects all outlets.
7. Work is finished by noon Monday and inspector approves and signs off on permits.
8. Open on Tuesday.

Permits—Drywall

The work may get done after hours when the barbershop is closed or during a few hours every evening. It all depends on how extensive the work is. Two things you must be aware of concerning permits when working on partitions or building rooms:

1. The room or partition can only be built on one side and cannot be closed until you have approval from the framing inspector.
2. If there is any electrical or plumbing going in the wall, you will need a "rough" inspection before you close up the other side.

Once these inspections are approved, you can close up the wall and finish the room or partition. This just needs to be coordinated. You might be able to handle all of this while you are open—it all depends on the scope of the work. Discuss this with your contractor to strategize the best approach.

A Transformation Weekend

Many barbershop owners decide not to pull permits for the work they are doing. A lot of the work may be cosmetic and the subcontractors they use are licensed, but the barbershop owner may get talked out of plans and permits because of the delay. Ready, Set, Go! recommends pulling permits, but if you decide not to, please use a licensed subcontractor, not a handyman with talent. Below is a step-by-step process on how to handle this transformation so you can reopen as soon as possible.

Before You Get Started

Hopefully, you decided to consult a professional in the industry to help guide you with the equipment/furniture you purchased. Many design companies that specialize in this industry give you a space-plan, drawings, and specifications on everything you purchased. Just before the work begins, we recommend a group meeting with all the subcontractors and your designer. Have all of the drawings and specifications on hand for all to review and ask questions. Coordinate a schedule so everyone is on the same path and understands the schedule completely. Hopefully, the equipment/furniture is at the location and everyone can see exactly what is involved. Your old furniture must be considered in the transformation process. You may need to arrange to dispose of it or it may have some value. In that case, you may be able to trade it in to the furniture company to help offset the cost of your new furniture or sell it on your own. Get rid of it at any price. If not, it will cost you to move it.

Here are some recommended selling prices for your used equipment:

- Barber chairs: $125 to $250 depending on make, model, and condition
- Styling chairs: $25 to $50 depending on make, model, and condition
- Dryer chair: $35 to $50
- Reception Desk: small (4 to 5 feet), $50 to $100; large desk, $100 to $500
- Shampoo sinks: $25; if they are marble or porcelain style, $50 to $75
- Shampoo chairs: $25
- Freestanding sink units: $50 to $100; if they are European or were expensive when new, $100 to $300
- Styling stations: simple stations, $10 to $25. Freestanding or custom units, $50 to $200
- Nail tables: $25 to $50
- Nail stools: $10
- Pedicure unit: $50 to $100 for base model; for motorized unit, $250 to $500
- Facial tables: standard style, $25 to $75; for a hydraulic or electric style, $100 to $500
- Skin care unit: $100 to $300
- Reception chairs: $10 to $50
- Retail units: $25 to $300
- Mirrors: $10 to $25
- Barber poles: $50 to $200
- Dispensary cabinets: anything

These prices can vary widely. Remember, you are giving these people good prices as long as they are willing to pick up the equipment or furniture on your schedule and timeline. If you don't trade it in or sell it, you need to haul it away and that will cost hundreds of dollars.

Preparation

Put up a sign well in advance to let your clients know when you are remodeling; be sure to include closed and reopen dates on the sign. It is also good to show the new design and some of the new equipment and furniture on a presentation board; this will excite clients and staff. Several of your staff will give their opinion on the furniture, including their likes and dislikes. Be diplomatic. But, remember, this is your business and it's what YOU want to do. Book your last appointment early Friday or Saturday afternoon (depending on when you need to be closed) and have your staff ready.

The Start

1. Have boxes for each staff member to clean out their station. Have them bring the box home or store it somewhere on the premises out of the way.

2. Have the front desk team do the same process and clean out the front desk. Also, mark the boxes for all your retail and try to keep it organized for restocking the shelves.

3. Bring your computer person in to unhook and pack your credit card processor and computer system so they can reinstall it when ready and not misplace any cables or wires.

Now the Real Fun Begins

1. Tear out all unwanted furniture, cabinets, chairs, pedicure units—whatever you are remodeling—and have your barber equipment/furniture company or "buyers" pick it up. Try to clear the space as much as possible so your installers or contractors are not tripping over each other.

2. For the tear-out, your electrician and plumber will need to be there to unhook the existing sinks and any existing electrical that may be attached to the old cabinets.

3. Your plumber and electrician will start modifying plumbing or electrical for the new equipment/furniture.

4. At the same time, bring in all of the new equipment/furniture for installation. Try to work in places that are not in the way of the plumber or electrician.

5. Coordinate with the subcontractors on hooking everything up.

6. Once everything is installed, call your staff to set up their stations or department.

7. Call your computer person to hook up your system and credit card terminal.

8. As everything is being set up, you can do any light assembly work, such as building the barber chairs or dryer chairs. These items are very simple to put together.

9. Set up your retail, clean the barbershop, and get ready to open in the morning.

What we described can be done in a four-day period, closing late Saturday afternoon, and opening up on Thursday for business. All you need is good coordination and good subcontractors who are committed to getting your project done and your barbershop reopened in a timely manner.

We recently remodeled Jon Lori Salon in Fair Haven, New Jersey. The shop owner had the commitment described above and did a complete facelift over a four-day period. The installation crew worked until 2:00 a.m. the day they reopened. A cleaning crew came in at 3:00 a.m. and they were finished and ready to reopen by 9:00 a.m. The secret was hard work and dedication from everyone involved.

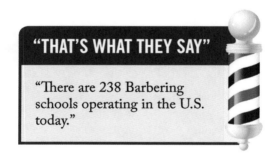

"THAT'S WHAT THEY SAY"

"There are 238 Barbering schools operating in the U.S. today."

Things to remember when starting your remodeling project:

- ◯ Let clients know about what's going on and what to expect.

- ◯ If you have a plan for a new design and layout, frame and display it for all to see.

- ◯ Plan for delays. Murphy's Law may or may not strike your barbershop remodel project, but anticipate delays.

- ◯ If money is needed from your banker, work out all details before you think about starting your remodel project.

- ◯ Box all things that may be in the way of contractors and equipment/furniture installers.

- ◯ Plan your all clients' appointments around work schedules.

- ◯ Plan that major construction or your new equipment/furniture install during the evening or when you are closed over the weekend.

THE GOOD, THE BAD & THE UGLY

(Brought to you by barbershop and salon owners and other industry leaders)

Sue Gahr, Owner of Studio 2 Hair Salon, Point Pleasant, NJ

"The best part of remodeling the salon I bought from my former employer was now having the ability to add what I felt would make the salon "me!" I wanted my clients to feel welcome and comfortable. I wanted a salon that I could call home and be proud of. When I was finished with my remodel, that's exactly how it was. My clients are happy and so am I. The worst part was realizing I had to get rid of nails. I needed the room for my hair business. The person I had to let go was a friend and colleague. I know a lot about hair and color, that is my passion. I knew nothing about nails. I had to let it go."

Thomas Gilhooley, Get It Together Hair and Nail Salon, Houston, TX

"The worst thing I did was not have a budget. What started as a small remodel turned into a three-month project. My budget was blown and, because I didn't plan well, it cost me a fortune with my contractor. Plan, budget, and put a timeline together—don't do it without these three things. Plus, I had no idea custom equipment could take as long as 10 to 12 weeks to get made. That killed me."

PART III

FINANCING

———

CHAPTER 30

Leasing for the Life of Your Business

"Money can't buy happiness, it can, however, rent it."

—Anonymous

Have you ever heard of sweat equity? It's the labor that you put into your own projects. As you move closer to opening or revamping your salon, you're going to invest a lot of sweat equity into getting it right.

In addition to sweat equity, you'll be investing a lot of finances into your business. Savings, loans, gifts from family and friends, sure, all of these will give you a little of what you need, but where do you turn when the bank says "No" to your loan application? How do you pay for the fixtures, equipment and installation? Where do you turn?

You turn to a lease finance company.

For years, distributors and manufacturers in the beauty industry have known about furniture and equipment leasing as a financing option, but only in the last 15 years or so have smaller salons taken advantage of this type of financing.

Here are 10 reasons why you, as a salon owner, should use leasing as a financial tool in place of conventional bank financing.

Bank vs. Lease Finance Company

In order to be approved at your local bank, the applicant must submit three years of personal and corporate tax returns with a completed loan application. The corporate returns must show a profit in order or the bank to consider lending any money to the business. Leasing companies require an application that is typically reviewed the same day it is received and can be approved for up to $75,000. The process is quite different from traditional, tedious bank loans. In fact, more than 90% of salons wouldn't qualify for a conventional bank loan in today's business environment because most fail to show a profit (or show a very small profit when they do). For a lease finance company to consider you a good candidate, you need to meet minimum qualifications, but a lot of the decision rests on your credit score. We cannot emphasize enough: You must have a great credit score.

Startup Financing

Without a minimum of two years of continual operation, most banks won't consider extending credit to your salon. So how are you supposed to finance a startup?

Typically the only lender willing to extend financing to startup salon businesses are those with a niche expertise in a particular line of equipment or industry. Therefore, if you are a new salon owner, leasing may be your best bet and may well be the most competitive option for obtaining new furniture and equipment. Your furniture and equipment sales representatives will be able to help you identify a company that fits your needs.

Establish Business Credit

To be considered for a business loan, your business needs to have a credit record. Lease financing establishes that credit as you make your on-time payments. As your business grows, you'll need to acquire new equipment and furniture to meet increased demand and fill the salon space. By establishing your credit with a lease company, it becomes easier to purchase your next piece of furniture or equipment or expand, relocate or remodel your salon.

Home vs. Equipment

The only collateral pledged on an equipment lease is the equipment. There's a 0% chance of losing your home due to payment default. Lease companies don't ask for personal collateral, which leaves you, your family, your possessions and the life you've built out of the frying pan if your business didn't go as planned.

Quick Turnaround

If opening your own business or your remodel project is like most, it will run over budget, which can exhaust your cash supply or leave you short handed, which makes opening on time and fully equipped, stocked and staffed a difficult prospect. Equipment lease financing lets you avoid a lengthy approval process so you can get everything ordered and installed in a matter of weeks. Upon receipt of your credit application and lease quote (how much you'd like to borrow), most lease companies will respond with approval, rejection or a request for additional information within 24 hours.

Conserve Your Money

Lease financing allows you to conserve your money, which you can utilize elsewhere in your business. Leasing offers you a predictable payment to fit into your budget. The fixed repayment price won't fluctuate like many traditional business loans, and the interest rate will stay the same for the life of the lease.

Down Payment

Equipment lease financing does not require a large down payment, which is the normal case for traditional loans. You can expect to put down 10% or less of the equipment lease as a security deposit.

Tax Advantages

Leasing offers you the ability to write off lease payments. Depending on the terms of your lease payment agreement, you may be able to subtract the payment as an expense for the life of the agreement. A bank loan doesn't offer this write-off. Take advantage of the recently modified IRS Section 179, which enables businesses to write off thousands of dollars of leased equipment every year.

Avoid Obsolescence

Technology and designs are always changing, including new equipment for processing color, display cases, salon software and other tools you need. Why should you be stuck with outdated equipment that puts you at a competitive disadvantage? With equipment financing, you can obtain the new technology and keep your salon out in front of the competition.

Going Out of Business

In the event of default, the lease agreement usually indicated the lessor will repossess the leased equipment and resell it for fair market value. This is different from a bank loan. Default on that and the bank simply holds an auction and asks for the balance due. They have no interest in reselling equipment or wanting you to succeed.

Today there are a handful of lease companies (Quest Resources and Castleton Capital, among others) that focus on your niche – the beauty industry. You may find it easier to discuss your salon's needs with a lease company that has an ongoing relationship with equipment and furniture manufacturers and distributors.

Above everything else, you'll enjoy the process of working with a company who has an understanding of the beauty industry as well as the needs of salons similar to yours. They have the knowledge, passion and resources at their disposal to help set you up for success.

When Lease Financing Equipment or Retail Furniture, Remember to Ask:

- Do you own the equipment at the end of the term?
- Are you responsible to have insurance on the leased equipment?
- Who maintains the equipment?
- Can you give the equipment away or sell it at the end of the term?
- Who is responsible for the tax on the sale of the equipment?

CHAPTER 31

Start-Up Expense Worksheet

Below is a breakdown of expenses you may incur. If they do not apply, leave them blank.

Item & Area	Expense
Construction	
Permits	
Impact fees (from the city)	
Architect plans	
Designer	
Rent (first, last, and security deposit)	
Barbershop sign	
Barber pole	
Barbershop furniture	
Barbershop front desk computer	
a. Software program	
b. Copier/printer	

(Spreadsheet is continued on next page)

(Spreadsheet is continued from previous page)

Item & Area	Expense
Office furniture	
a. Desk and chair	
b. Computer	
c. Copier/printer	
Business license (city and state)	
a. Lawyer	
b. Accountant	
Business insurance	
Utility deposits	
a. Water	
b. Electric	
c. Telephone/internet service	
d. Garbage (may be included with location)	
Advertising	
a. Website	
b. Social marketing	
c. Magazines	
d. City or county contributions	
e. Web hosting or domain name	
Initial retial and barbershop supplies	
Misc. expenses (approx. 7%)	
TOTAL	

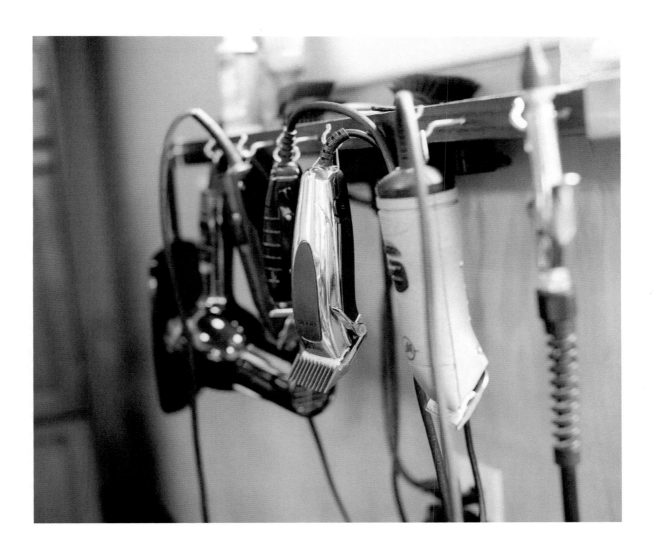

CHAPTER 32

The Money Hunt

"The lack of money is the root of all evil."

—Mark Twain

Where can you find business startup money? When it comes to financing these days, it is more difficult than ever to find a bank that has the resources and willingness to lend to a small business. Given certain economic conditions, achieving the American Dream and one day owning your own barbershop may prove to be extremely difficult. You may have all the skills, education, drive, and personality, but lack one very important aspect—money!

The money factor puts limitations on any new business venture and destroys dreams. If you are lucky enough to either borrow from family members or have your own personal savings, that's great. But, these options can put you in a compromising position.

If opening your own barbershop is your dream, don't be discouraged. Financial alternatives can assist you in not only making this a reality, but a success.

How Deep Are Your Pockets?

The idea of financing your new business may be daunting at first glance, but it's the most popular source of business startup money. First, look at what you have available and what you could easily liquidate:

- How much cash do you have in your bank accounts?
- What assets can you sell? (Cars, jewelry—gold and silver are now at an all-time highs—and antiques).
- Do you have a stock portfolio you can leverage?
- Can you draw equity from real estate or a home that you own?

211

Family & Friends

The second most popular source of business startup money is from family and friends. They may be willing to provide a business startup loan or an outright gift due to the fact they believe in you and your business plan. The advantages of a personal loan or gift are that it eliminates the bank paperwork, credit approval process, and bank fees. A major drawback is that if the business falters your relationship with family or friends may not survive. It will certainly cause tension and negativity at the next family function.

Credit Cards

A recent study stated that over 54 percent of businesses use credit cards in some capacity to get up and running. Credit cards provide instant money, and you can deduct the interest you pay if what you purchase is a business expense. Remember, easy money is harder to pay back. Most credit card money is lent at about 15 to 19 percent. Opening a business with this type of money can put you in a downward tailspin with no way out.

Life Insurance Policy

If you hold a whole life insurance policy with at least three years of maturity, you can likely get a loan against the cash value of your policy. Most insurance companies will lend you up to 90 percent of your policy's cash value at rates generally more attractive than those charged by credit card companies. You must continue to keep up with your premium payments on your policy.

Retirement Plan

Still working for someone else while starting your business? Then, check into borrowing against your 401(k). While rules vary, you can generally borrow half of what you have put into your retirement plan, up to a maximum of $50,000. The drawback is that when taking out the money, you will be penalized 10 percent and you will have to pay the taxes on the amount you take out of the 401(k).

Finding Funding on the Web

The Internet has changed how business startups find new business funding. Numerous sites on the Web offer advice about how to put together a business plan and connect you with various sources that can help you find the money needed to go forward with your business plan.

Here are some reference sites:

- www.bizoffice.com
- www.businessfinance.com
- www.fundingpost.com

The sites listed above allow you to search for funding sources and access business guidelines. These sites will navigate you through a step-by-step guide to creating, supporting, and presenting your funding request.

Bank Loans

Many things are changing when it comes to banking and the overall economy. We are experiencing layoffs in every industry, and job security is almost impossible to find. The lure of private enterprise is now more interesting for many who have been laid off or decided on a career change for their future. The American Dream is still possible and, yes, you still can get money at your local bank—but at what cost?

Bank loans are tough for any new startups to acquire. Usually, banks loan money to companies that are stable and profitable and that have been in business more than three years. Banks will also look for owners who have a proven track record and business background. Loans from banks are not impossible to obtain, but the requirements these days are far more difficult. We will discuss the approval procedure later in this chapter.

SBA Financing

Depending on your credit record and the strength of your business plan, you may be able to secure a Small Business Administration (SBA) loan. An SBA loan is guaranteed by the government and usually has a better interest rate than a conventional bank loan. Most bank loans are five year, whereas SBA loans can be as long as ten years. The longer payback term is helpful to a new business venture and certainly takes the burden off of paying back the loan over a shorter period. It will make the first few years of business much easier to not have a large loan payment every month. The downside of working with the SBA is that the application process is very tedious, the completion process intense, and the approval process can take up to six months before you get a response on your loan status.

More recently, SBA loans for $5,000 to $50,000 have become attainable that provide an approval process of less than two weeks.

- www.strategiesforsmallbusiness.com
- www.sba.gov

Home Equity

If you own your home, you can take out a home equity loan, a second mortgage, or refinance your original mortgage. You can borrow as much as 80 percent of your home's equity. The most important thing to remember when you borrow against your home is, if your business should fail, the bank will foreclose on your home unless you have the means to pay it back. (This option is discussed in detail later in the chapter.)

Leasing

Leasing sources can accommodate all applicants for financing whether you are in business 20 years or a new startup barbershop. Leasing programs give you the flexibility to finance your furniture, equipment, and installation. The application is less tedious than working with conventional banks. Once you fill out a lease application, you should have an answer within 72 hours. The leasing company does not put liens on your house or other assets. If you have been declined by a bank, you may find it worthwhile to try a leasing company.

- Quest Resources
- Castleton Capital

Government-Related Startup Programs

Many government operated organizations promote economic development and provide assistance to help particular types of people succeed in business. Often, this assistance includes financial support, such as startup business loans. Each state has programs that may be beneficial in a startup business. There are also many women's organizations throughout the country that assist women who are trying to open a business.

Partnership

Partners can be a great source of financing support for a startup barbershop business. You will have additional capital and benefit from the skills and experience another individual brings to your business. A partnership may include financial support or being able to share responsibilities of running the day-to-day operations of the business. Conversely, you will have to share profits. But, if the business does not work out, you will have to terminate your partnership and most likely your friendship will not survive.

Money is an important aspect for your business to succeed. Being able to obtain it without the restrictions of giving up your business or putting your house up as collateral is not going to be an easy task. Obtaining money with high interest rates will not make it easy for you in the early stages of opening a business.

How to Get a "YES" From Your Banker

Proper preparation and knowing the correct answers to the most common banking questions often determines whether your bank gives you a yes or a no answer when you apply for a loan. The best way to prepare is to be ready to answer all objections.

Bankers most commonly reject a loan for one of five reasons. However, it is possible to overcome them and get approved if you follow the suggestions in the next section.

1. No sound business plan
2. Not knowing the exact amount of money you need and what it will be used for

3. Not showing the ability to pay back the loan
4. Poor credit worthiness
5. Little to no money in the bank

Effectively Informing the Bank About You & Your Business

Take these key steps to ensure that the loan officer is properly informed.

1. Put together a sound business plan. The plan can be a few pages, but it should be well thought out. The business plan shows the loan officer you have credibility as the owner and that you're not just rushing into something.

2. Be prepared to supply business credit references and your personal credit history. The applicant must have a proven track record in repaying distributors and suppliers. It is also important that all personal obligations (mortgages, car loans, student loans, and credit cards) be paid in a timely manner. If you have a history of slow payment on any of these, you must have a sufficient explanation in writing or your loan request will be immediately denied. Good personal and business credit policies are the keys to success!

3. Provide a brief description of the barbering and men's grooming industry, including the average and top salaries of barbers and the projected annual revenue for your barbershop. Use industry magazines and special publications. Remember, most bankers are unaware our industry has grown into a multibillion dollar profession. The bank has to feel confident that the grooming industry is professional and has the potential for growth. Unfortunately, the reputation of our industry has been tarnished by individuals who have not run their business on a professional level. But, the barbering and men's grooming industry has come a long way in the past 10 years. Therefore, educate your banker on how profitable the barbering and men's grooming industry really is.

4. Share your education and experience in running a business and your support structure. If you've taken classes at a local college, get letters of recommendation from your instructors. Show the bank your performance record in school. If you have held a management position in a barbershop or hair salon, provide them with a letter of recommendation and share how you improved the performance of the business during your term in the management position. If you can, put together an advisory board of people you know who are willing to help you get your business off the ground. Most of us know people in marketing, business management, accounting, etc., and they may be willing to meet with you as a favor to give you free advice.

State Why You Need the Money

When a loan officer asks you how much money you need to borrow, don't reply with, "How much will you loan me?" While preparing for your loan, conduct an in-depth analysis of your borrowing needs and stipulate whether you're starting a new business or remodeling/expanding an existing business. You must have all of your costs outlined and on paper before going to a loan officer. The worksheet in CHAPTER 29: Start-Up Expense Worksheet will be helpful. By creating a business plan, you should get an idea of how much operating capital you will need to open and operate throughout the early months.

Do Your Numbers Support the Loan Request?

If your business has been at a break-even point, or even losing money, there's still hope. However, it won't be easy. Bankers are trained to make decisions based primarily on a company's ability to generate sufficient cash flow through consistent profitability. If you have lost money, you need to know the reason for the loss. The loss may be caused by the economy, poor health, labor problems, or the weather! Hurricane Katrina is an example of this. Banks understood the unforeseen catastrophe and modified many loans. The bank will want to know what changes the owner will make to fix these problems, if possible.

The most important thing the bank is looking for is the income and profit you are reporting on your tax returns. Remember, hiding income from Uncle Sam when filing your taxes will only hurt you when applying for a business loan. Also, keep in mind loan officers never want to hear, "My tax return doesn't reflect what I actually make." Such a statement will not give the right impression and not reporting income is illegal. It will guarantee a decline.

What Type of Collateral Do You Have?

Small business owners complain that lenders lack an adequate understanding of the market value of assets such as furniture, equipment, and inventory (retail and supplies). And, they are right! Bankers aren't experts on most of the collateral given, no matter what is being pledged. Banks will generally lend no more than 80 percent of the value of real estate/equipment.

You may have personal assets, such as debt-free automobiles, bank certificates, stocks, or real estate that could be used to secure the loan. It is guaranteed the bank will ask you to secure your entire business and will usually look for other avenues outside the business, as well as personal assets, for collateral. You must address these issues before applying for your loan. An unsecured loan is almost impossible in today's banking world.

Personal Guarantee(s)

Most banks won't lend to any business without personal guarantees from the owner(s). The purpose of a guarantee is to provide a secondary repayment source for the loan in the event the small business is unable to pay. What this means is, if you borrow $10,000 and default on the loan, the bank will go after you, personally, for the remaining loan. If you don't have the money, they have the right to seize any personal assets that equal the amount of the loan.

As a matter of policy, banks ask for personal guarantees from the owner(s). The guarantee demonstrates a full commitment on your part, which will enhance your chances for loan approval.

Applying for a small business loan is not an easy process. Banks are not in the business to lose money; that's why their procedures have become so arduous. They do not want any risky propositions. However, if you are prepared to answer these common inquiries from bankers, you will improve your chances of obtaining the financing you need.

Good preparation and showing confidence in your ideas as an owner will help establish the credibility necessary to convince the banker you have business smarts and what it takes to run a business.

Using Your Home as Collateral

Most first-time business owners are so sure they will succeed in their business, some are willing to put up their biggest asset as collateral—their "Home Sweet Home!"

Banks, by nature, are very conservative. Now more than ever, they are extremely cautious when lending money, especially for a new business. They feel the risk is so high for a new business that they will ask you for personal assets such as a pledged 401(k), life insurance policy, bank certificates, stocks, or any debt-free real estate to secure a startup business loan, not to mention the personal guarantee of every person involved with the business.

If you are considering pledging your home as collateral, be aware of what could happen if your business should fail. We are sure the worst feeling in the world would be for you to receive a phone call letting you know that your home is now being seized because you pledged it for your new business loan. The other way the bank will notify you is when the local sheriff comes and stops by your house with a warrant letting you know that your house is being seized because of default on your loan payments. It is not a game and should not be taken lightly.

Generally, banks try to negotiate a new payment plan when they see your business is in trouble. This will allow you to pay the debt back gradually, without being asked to leave your home. The bank's position, as far as personal residences and businesses go, is to try and work with the borrower or guarantor as much as possible. Banks look at homes as a last resort. They are not in the real estate business nor do they want to be. Banks do not want to retain assets, especially residential real estate. But you must be realistic. You pledged your home as collateral, and if you are forced to close your business, they will take your home. Beware of the consequences!

Currently, the value of business assets amounts to 10 to 20 cents on the dollar when auctioned off. After the entire barbershop business and all of the assets are auctioned off, the bank will look to the borrowers to find a way to settle the remaining debt. At this point, you will wish you never opened your business and pledged your home.

When a bank accepts a home as collateral on a startup business loan, they put a lien on the home for the entire value of the loan amount borrowed, even if the debt is more than the homeowner's equity. The bank's philosophy is that, in time, the equity will increase through appreciation of the home over the length of the business loan. The bank's lien will be a secondary lien behind the primary mortgage holder.

If the business should fail, it doesn't necessarily mean that the home has to be sold to settle your debt or that you will be evicted from your home. If the homeowner has enough equity, then you can refinance the mortgage, use this equity to pay off the balance of the business loan with the bank, and get the lien removed and keep your home.

The people whose businesses fail and don't have enough equity in their homes, or have additional debt, may opt for personal bankruptcy. Typically, this allows the borrower to work out a repayment plan and avoid losing his home to satisfy creditors.

Bankruptcy is actually the most common course of action borrowers take. They try just about anything to save their business and home. They will borrow from family members, run up credit card debt, and borrow against virtually every other asset they have.

At this point, they have usually defaulted on their business loan, incurred significant debt from vendors, credit cards and state/federal taxes. It's not just the bank that has not been paid, but a whole barrage of creditors. When this happens, it is hopeless to continue the business.

Most banks speak to the business owners on a regular basis. In most cases, the borrower is required to give an annual update on the business with their tax returns. The key is to have open communications with your bank. If you see that you are having difficulties with the business, notify the bank as early as possible. A monthly visit with your accountant will also help you with bookkeeping and keep your business records up to date and on time. It is better to be proactive with your bank when you see that you're having financial difficulty.

Going into business has great rewards, this is true. However, not all of us are always so fortunate. Remember, putting up your home should be your very last resort. Never give what can't be given back.

Leasing for the Life of Your Business

Most entrepreneurs start businesses with sweat equity and their savings. In many cases, the barbershop owner runs short of monies due to cost overruns. It seems like Murphy's Law always strikes halfway through the project. Your architect or interior designer informs you that the electrical system isn't adequate or the plumbing is too old to fix, or the city is requiring a one-time impact fee for water.

The total cost of your project is now over budget $10,000 to $15,000, and you still haven't ordered your sign. If your local bank did not approve your loan, then leasing may be an alternative.

Distributors and manufacturers in the hair, beauty, and men's grooming industry are aware of these bank hang-ups and explored other financing options (i.e., leasing) to help their potential clients obtain the money to purchase their barbershop furniture and equipment.

Listed below are ten reasons why barbershop owners should use leasing as a financing tool, as opposed to conventional bank financing.

Bank vs. Lease Finance Company

In order to get approved at your local bank, the applicant must submit three years of personal and corporate tax returns with a completed application. The corporate returns must show a profit in order for the bank to even consider lending you any money. Leasing companies require that you fill out an application. That application is usually reviewed the same day it is submitted and can be approved up to $75,000. The process is quite different from the tedious bank loan application process. It's a fact that over 90 percent of barbershops would not qualify for the conventional bank loan in today's business environment because most barbershops fail to show profits and a new business has no financial history to bring to the table when asking for a loan. Good personal credit is the driving force for obtaining an approval.

Startup Financing

Most banks may not consider extending credit if your barbershop does not have a minimum of two years in business. The only lenders (typically leasing companies) who will supply financing to startup barbershops and other similar hair, beauty, and spa business are those with a niche expertise in the industry or a particular line of equipment/furniture. Therefore, if you are a new business owner, working with a leasing may be your best and most competitive option for obtaining your new furniture and equipment. Your furniture and equipment salespeople will be able to point you in the right direction.

Establish Business Credit

By financing your equipment/furniture through a leasing company, you can quickly establish business credit if you are a new or existing barbershop. As your business grows, you will need to either trade up or acquire new furniture and equipment to meet your increased demand. By establishing your credit with a lease company, it will be easier to purchase your next piece of furniture or equipment or expand, relocate, or remodel your barbershop.

Home vs. Equipment

The only collateral pledged on an equipment lease is the equipment you are purchasing. The lease finance company will not ask for any other items to be pledged, such as a major asset or your personal residence, building, car, or your business itself. Conversely, it is nearly impossible to get a business loan from your neighborhood bank without pledging your home or a major asset as collateral.

Quick Turnaround

If your business or remodel project is like most, you will run over budget and exhaust your cash supply before you have everything you need to open or reopen. Equipment lease financing allows you to avoid a lengthy approval process so that you can get your furniture and equipment ordered and installed within just a few weeks. Upon receipt of your credit application and equipment quotation, you can expect a rapid response and approval within 24 hours.

Conserve Your Money

Lease financing allows you to conserve your money, which you can utilize elsewhere in your business. Leasing is a predictable budgetary tool since payments are fixed and not subject to the fluctuations of a business loan that may go up with an increase in interest rates.

NOTE

All bank loan payments are different, they may fluctuate monthly. Your monthly lease payment will always be the same, which is better for budgeting.

Down Payment

Equipment lease financing does not require a large down payment, which is the normal case with bank loans. You can expect to put down 10 percent or less of the equipment lease as a security deposit.

Tax Advantages

Leasing offers the ability to write off your lease payments. Depending on your lease option, you may be able to subtract your lease payment as an expense every month for the term of the lease. A bank loan does not offer this write-off. Take advantage of the recently modified IRS Section 179 enabling businesses to write off thousands of dollars of leased equipment per year.

Avoid Obsolescence

Technology and designs are always changing, including new equipment for processing color, display cases, and software (to help you effectively run your barbershop). Why should you be stuck with old and dated equipment? They can put your barbershop at a competitive disadvantage. Equipment financing allows you to receive the benefit of new equipment and technology today, while paying for it with tomorrow's dollars.

Going Out of Business

In the event of default, the lease agreement usually indicates that the lessor will repossess the leased equipment and resell it for its fair market value. It is very different from a bank loan, because if you default on your loan, the bank would have no interest in the equipment or reselling it on your behalf. However, the entire outstanding balance will be due to the bank and the asset(s) pledged (such as your home) can be seized.

Today, there are only a handful of lease companies (mentioned previously) that focus on your niche—the hair, beauty, and men's grooming industry. You may find it easier to discuss your needs with a lease company who constantly works with the equipment and furniture manufacturers or distributors. The process will enable you to work with a company who has a true understanding of the industry, as well as your needs regarding the furniture and equipment you are purchasing and the cost to install it.

THE GOOD, THE BAD & THE UGLY

(Brought to you by barbershop and salon owners and other industry leaders)

Dukes Barber Shop, Staten Island, NY

"Cash is king! I saved for 5 years to make sure I had enough capital to open my business and cover expenses for one year. Having cash made it easy and I wasn't relying on a bank or financial institution as backup."

DeAnne Vaughan

"Making sure I had enough capital. Getting [too] busy with build-out, ordering product, etc. You need to have some in reserve and have an estimated spending plan. I also think start small and then build bigger."

PART IV

APPENDICES

———

APPENDIX 1

Timeline

ONE YEAR (or more) BEFORE OPENING

- Look at the pros and cons of owning and operating your own barbershop
- Decide if you are ready
- Take the entrepreneurial self-test
- Will you buy an existing barbershop or start your own?
- Decide if you will rent booths

BUYING AN EXISTING BARBERSHOP

- Analyze the operation
- Review financials
- Create a spreadsheet with projections and debt ratios
- Create a budget
- Make an offer to purchase
- Remodel the barbershop
- Hire and architect and contractor
- Determine your list of priorities for coordination and timing
- Begin your transformation weekend

STARTING A NEW BARBERSHOP

- Choose a business structure
- Name your barbershop
- Hire a lawyer

- Gather/apply for:
    - EIN (Employer Identification Number)
    - Articles of Incorporation
    - Resolution
    - Identification
    - Initial deposit
- Pick a location for your new barbershop
- Complete the startup expense worksheet
- Work on your new business checklists: business plan, incorporation, etc.
- SECURE START-UP FUNDS!!
- Negotiate your lease
- Find a barbershop designer and an architect
- Price your barbershop furniture/equipment
- Find your contractor
- Set up a business checking account
- Plan your signage
- Choose the colors of your barbershop
- Obtain business insurance
- Hire a bookkeeper or accountant
- Design and develop web presence and determine social marketing strategy
- Decide on computers and software for your barbershop
- Choose a business phone system
- Write your employee manual
- Design and develop a barbershop menu
- Setup online promotions
- Choose which retail products to sell
- Begin to hire

WITHIN SIX MONTHS OF OPENING

- Plan barbershop promotions and loyalty programs
- Discreetly begin the hiring process

WITHIN THREE MONTHS OF OPENING

- Arrange for barbershop promotions and loyalty programs (negotiate with vendors, decide if you need loyalty cards, etc.)

WITHIN ONE MONTH OF OPENING

- Train staff on computer software and hardware

WITHIN TWO OR THREE WEEKS OF OPENING

- The controversial exit
- Preparing for the open house

AFTER OPENING

- Successful retail in year one
- Surviving the first year—what to expect and how to adjust
- Build your business to sell
- Moving your barbershop

New Barbershop Checklist

○ Define your business plan (Goal setting, clientele, demographics, etc.).

○ Meet with your realtor.

○ Site location with good visibility and easy access.

○ Review preliminary lease. Is potential site zoned for a barbershop?

○ Prepare estimated annual income projection.

○ Preliminary budget plan.

○ Preliminary design & floor plan with supplier of furnishings, architect, or designer.

○ Design logo for barbershop (designer or graphic artist).

○ Write barbershop policies, employee and front desk manual.

○ Meet with your attorney to discuss setting up corporation and lease as well as items.

○ Meet with your banker to discuss items.

○ Meet with your accountant. Discuss purchase vs. leasing, bookkeeping vs. computer software, etc.

○ Select furniture and color scheme for your barbershop.

○ Set up delivery date for the equipment.

○ Cash register, computer system or bookkeeping/software system.

○ Barbershop intercom and/or music system.

○ Finalize barbershop design and floor plan.

○ Pick out flooring, wall coverings, lighting, accent pieces, etc.

◯ Meet with architect for complete set of plans. Barbershop meets all city and state codes.

◯ Obtain bids for construction, usually with general contractor(s).

◯ Sign lease, order barbershop furnishings and hire contractor(s).

◯ Arrange for electric, gas, water, phone service/internet provider and trash removal.

◯ Plan opening date (make allowances for any delays).

◯ Order dispensary and retail supplies and products.

◯ Plan opening advertising (Yellow Pages, Internet listings, Facebook, local newspapers, direct mail, etc.).

◯ Order magazines for customers.

◯ Design and order outside sign in compliance with lease.

◯ Order towels for shampoo area (special colors).

◯ Barbershop price list on "Menu" of services.

◯ Design customer sales tickets & service record files.

◯ Order appointment cards, business cards, stamps and pads, stationary and envelopes.

◯ Interview potential employees.

◯ Set up payroll company.

◯ Order plants or plant service and outside doormats if applicable.

◯ Order washer and dryer and laundry supplies or arrange for towel service.

◯ Arrange for credit card charge plate machine or Merchant Processing with your bank.

◯ Arrange for vending machines if applicable.

◯ Purchase bookkeeping record books, appointment book, pencils, pens and stapler.

◯ Purchase first aid kit, fire extinguisher, toilet paper and paper towel dispenser for restroom.

◯ Purchase file cabinet, file folders, vacuum cleaner, broom and dust pan.

◯ Purchase coffee bar supplies or arrange for coffee service.

◯ Purchase ashtrays, waste baskets, cleaning supplies or arrange for cleaning service.

◯ Plan Grand Opening- usually 30 days after opening.

◯ Arrange for all inspections.

◯ Ongoing advertising, promotions and employee training.

Industry Resource Guide

Quest Resources Inc.
Salon/Barber Equipment Finance Specialist, Creative Financing Solutions
    jgrissler@questrs.com
    www.questrs.com
    (800) 449-0777

Takara Belmont
Salon Equipment/Barbering Equipment
    www.takarabelmont.com
    (877) 283-1289

Collins Manufacturing
Salon/ Barbering Equipment
    info@collinsmfgco.com
    www.collinsmfgco.com
    (800)292-6450

Minerva Beauty
Salon/Barbering Equipment
    www.minervabeauty.com
    (888)332-0123

Teakettle Junction Productions
Salon and Barbershop Marketing, Writing
    Jason@TeakettleJunction.com
    www.teakettlejunction.com

Glossary

Build-out: estimate of the amount and location of potential development for an area.

Equity: the net value of assets minus liabilities.

Executive Summary: an overview of the main points of a business plan or proposal.

GM methodology: general merchandise methodology, or how you will purchase, display, and record your merchandise.

Lien: the legal claim of one person upon the property of another person to secure the payment of a debt or the satisfaction of an obligation.

Market-driven: determined by or responsive to market forces.

Non-compete Agreement: a contract that restricts participation in a certain market by a company or an individual under specific circumstances. Employers often require employees to sign a non-compete agreement to deter them from quitting or joining a competitor.

Point-of-Sale (POS): (also sometimes referred to as Point of Purchase (POP)) or checkout is the location where a transaction occurs. A "checkout" refers to a POS terminal or, more generally, to the hardware and software used for checkouts, the equivalent of an electronic cash register.

Prorate: to make an arrangement on a basis of proportional distribution.

Reserve requirements or hold-backs: requirements regarding the amount of funds that banks must hold in reserve against deposits made by their customers. This money must be in the bank's vaults or at the closest Federal Reserve Bank.

Revenue stream: a form of revenue. Revenue streams refer specifically to the individual methods by which money comes into a company.

SEO: Search Engine Optimization. This is the process of improving the visibility of a website in search engines via the "natural" or unpaid search results.

A **softphone** is a software program for making telephone calls over the Internet using a general purpose computer, rather than using dedicated hardware.

Twist-on wire connectors: used to fasten two or more electrical conductors together. They are a type of electrical connector.

UL (Underwriter's Laboratory): this company certifies electrical devices acceptable for USA use.

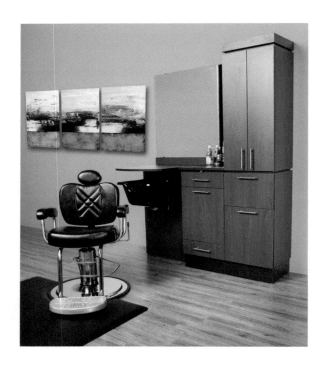

Special Thanks

Jeff and Eric would like to especially thank and acknowledge Patrick Parenty, L'Oreal, and their divisions for supporting Ready, Set, Go! and helping to make this one-of-a-kind publication a reality.

Contributors & Resources

Jeff Grissler, Quest Resources, Salon Equipment Financing (jgrissler@questrs.com). www.questrs.com

John Harms, President/Founder, Harms Software (Millennium). www.harms-software.com

Guy Wadas, National Sales Director, Integrity Payment Systems. www.integritypaymentsystems.com

Facebook Friends

Thank you for providing your stories and allowing us to share That's What They Say.*
Follow Jeff Grissler and Eric David Ryant on Facebook.

Image Sources

Takara Belmont – www.takarabelmont.com
Peter Millard Designs – www.millard-design.com
Rick Golden, Takara Belmont Design Specialist – rgolden@takarabelmont.com
Jeff Holmes, Takara Belmont Regional Manager – jholmes@takarabelmont.com
European Touch Pedicure Spas – www.europeantouch.com
Collins Manufacturing – www.collinsmfgco.com
Salon Centric Equipment Division – www.saloncentric.com

Editing and Production

B. Jason Frye, Writing and Editing
Teakettle Junction Productions
4642 Middlesex Road
Wilmington, North Carolina 28405

Interior Layout and Cover Design
Robin Krauss
Linden Design
www.lindendesign.biz

Business Resources

- Salon Consulting
- Design Layout and Plans
- School – Class Education
- Equipment Procurement
- Business Education

Jeff Grissler – jgrissler@questrs.com
Eric Ryant – ericryant@gmail.com

Quest Resources

Beauty Equipment Finance Specialists
We make your salon dreams possible.
www.questrs.com
800-449-0777

Follow Jeff and Eric on Facebook.

Visit us on the web at:
www.readysetgobooks.com
www.salonresourceguide.com

*Quotes provided via Facebook were offered freely by salon owners and without obligation or compensation from Ready, Set, Go! Publishing, its authors, contributors, or endorsers. Quotes used in this book follow "fair use" practices with proper attribution given to those who submitted comments. When content is offered via a public domain, such as Facebook, it means that those posting or commenting are allowing their posts or comments to be shared, used or accessed by people on and off of Facebook.